60 Promises to Pray over Your Daily Life

60 Promises to Pray over Your Daily Life

www.dayspring.com

First Edition, February 2017

Cover design by Kim Russell | Wahoo Designs

ISBN: 9781684089888

60 Promises to Pray over Your Daily Life

Table of Contents
Arranged by Topics

Introduction

God has made many promises to you, and He intends to keep every single one of them. His promises are found in a book like no other: the Holy Bible. The Lord's promises are eternal and unchanging, but in today's fast-paced world, circumstances can be so demanding and situations so confusing that it's easy to forget God's blessings and His mercy. This book is intended to remind you of the joy and the abundance that the Lord offers to all His children, including you.

Everyday life can be problematic at times, but no problems are too big for God. So, as you read these pages, please consider the power and the peace that can be yours when you turn everything over to Him.

This collection of prayers, Bible verses, and quotations addresses sixty topics of particular interest to Christian readers. May these pages be a blessing to you, and may you, in turn, be a blessing to those whom the Lord has seen fit to place along your path.

1

Abundance

The Promise of Abundance

I have come that they may have life,
and that they may have it more abundantly.

John 10:10 NKJV

Dear Lord, I thank You for the promise of abundance. Christ died so that I might have spiritual abundance here on earth and eternal life with Him in heaven. Keep me mindful of Christ's sacrifice and His love.

Today, Father, I will claim the joy that comes from the knowledge that You love me and that You will protect me, now and forever. Because You are my shepherd, I have nothing to fear.

I am grateful for the abundant life that Jesus promised. Grant me the wisdom to claim His blessings. And lead me, Lord, on Your path, today, tomorrow, and every day of my life.

Amen

More from God's Word

Until now you have asked for nothing in My name.
Ask and you will receive,
that your joy may be complete.

John 16:24 HCSB

Success, success to you, and success to those
who help you, for your God will help you . . .

I Chronicles 12:18 NIV

May Yahweh bless you and protect you; may Yahweh
make His face shine on you, and be gracious to you.

Numbers 6:24–25 HCSB

My cup runs over. Surely goodness and mercy
shall follow me all the days of my life;
and I will dwell in the house of the Lord forever.

Psalm 23:5–6 NKJV

And God is able to make all grace abound to you,
so that always having all sufficiency in everything,
you may have an abundance for every good deed.

II Corinthians 9:8 NASB

About Abundance

*God loves you and wants you to experience
peace and life—abundant and eternal.*

BILLY GRAHAM

*Knowing that your future is absolutely assured
can free you to live abundantly today.*

SARAH YOUNG

*We honor God by asking for great things when
they are a part of His promise. We dishonor Him
and cheat ourselves when we ask for molehills
where He has promised mountains.*

VANCE HAVNER

*God is the giver, and we are the receivers.
And His richest gifts are bestowed not upon those
who do the greatest things, but upon those
who accept His abundance and His grace.*

HANNAH WHITALL SMITH

A Timely Tip

God wants you to experience the kind of spiritual
abundance that only He can provide. When you stay
focused on His will, He will provide for your needs.

2

Acceptance

A Prayer for Acceptance

*Should we accept only good things from
the hand of God and never anything bad?*

Job 2:10 NLT

Dear Lord, You have promised that You have a plan for my life, a plan that is grander and more glorious than I can imagine. Because I trust You, Father, I can accept whatever life brings my way.

Today, let me focus on my blessings, not my disappointments. Let me accept what was, give thanks for what is, and have faith in what will be: the promise of eternal life with You.

This is the day that You have made, Lord. I will rejoice and be grateful for your plan, for your protection, and for Your love.

Amen

More from God's Word

Everything God made is good,
and nothing should
be refused if it is accepted with thanks.

I Timothy 4:4 NCV

Trust in the Lord with all your heart
and lean not on your own understanding.

Proverbs 3:5 NIV

For now we see in a mirror, dimly,
but then face to face. Now I know in part,
but then I shall know just as I also am known.

I Corinthians 13:12 NKJV

For the Lord is good, and His love is eternal;
His faithfulness endures through all generations.

Psalm 100:5 HCSB

He is the Lord. He will do what He thinks is good.

I Samuel 3:18 HCSB

About Acceptance

Christians who are strong in the faith grow as they accept whatever God allows to enter their lives.

BILLY GRAHAM

*Accept each day as it comes to you.
Do not waste your time and energy wishing
for a different set of circumstances.*

SARAH YOUNG

*Loving Him means the thankful acceptance
of all things that His love has appointed.*

ELISABETH ELLIOT

*One of the marks of spiritual maturity is the quiet
confidence that God is in control, without the need
to understand why He does what He does.*

CHARLES SWINDOLL

A Timely Tip

Once you accept the past—and make peace with it—you are free to live joyfully in the present. And that's precisely what you should do.

3

Action

Praying for the Courage to Do It Now

But prove yourselves doers of the word,
and not merely hearers who delude themselves.

JAMES 1:22 NASB

Dear Lord, You promise that my actions have consequences—let my actions always serve You. And You promise that hard work will be rewarded. Help me face my responsibilities now, not later.

When I am tempted to postpone important tasks, give me the wisdom and the courage to do my work. And let me follow closely in the footsteps of your Son, now and forever.

Today, Father, let me do my work and share your good news with friends, with family, and with the world.

Amen

More from God's Word

*For the kingdom of God
is not a matter of talk but of power.*

I Corinthians 4:20 HCSB

*Therefore, whenever we have the opportunity,
we should do good to everyone—
especially to those in the family of faith.*

Galatians 6:10 NLT

*Well done, good and faithful servant; you were
faithful over a few things, I will make you ruler
over many things. Enter into the joy of your lord.*

Matthew 25:21 NKJV

*When you make a vow to God, do not delay to fulfill it.
He has no pleasure in fools; fulfill your vow.*

Ecclesiastes 5:4 NIV

*Therefore, with your minds ready for action,
be serious and set your hope completely on the grace
to be brought to you at the revelation of Jesus Christ.*

I Peter 1:13 HCSB

About Taking Action

*Set yourself earnestly to see what you are made to do,
and then set yourself earnestly to do it.*

PHILLIPS BROOKS

*There is some task which the God of all the Universe,
the Great Creator, your Redeemer in Jesus Christ,
has for you to do—and which will remain undone
and incomplete until, by faith and obedience,
you step into the will of God.*

ALAN REDPATH

*Pray as though everything depended on God.
Work as though everything depended on you.*

ST. AUGUSTINE

The one word in the spiritual vocabulary is now.

OSWALD CHAMBERS

A Timely Tip

Procrastination is the enemy of progress. Don't let your enemy defeat you. If there's something you need to do today, then the best day to begin is this day. Tomorrow may be too late.

4

Adversity

A Prayer for Tough Time

I called to the LORD in my distress;
I called to my God.
From His temple He heard my voice,
and my cry for help reached his ears.

II SAMUEL 22:7 HCSB

Dear Lord, during difficult days, You have promised to give me strength. When I am fearful, You give me courage. When I am discouraged, You give me hope.

Let me live each day with the assurance that You are firmly in control, Father, and that Your love is sufficient to carry me above and beyond any challenge.

Give me the wisdom to treat my hardships as opportunities to trust You more. And give me an eternal perspective, a firm understanding that my troubles are temporary, but Your love endures forever.

Amen

More from God's Word

We are hard-pressed on every side, yet not crushed;
we are perplexed, but not in despair.

II Corinthians 4:8 NKJV

God blesses those who patiently endure testing.
Afterward they will receive the crown of life
that God has promised to those who love him.

James 1:12 NLT

The Lord is my shepherd; I shall not want.

Psalm 23:1 KJV

He heals the brokenhearted
and binds up their wounds.

Psalm 147:3 HCSB

The Lord is my rock, my fortress, and my deliverer,
my God, my mountain where I seek refuge.
My shield, the horn of my salvation,
my stronghold, my refuge, and my Savior.

II Samuel 22:2–3 HCSB

About Adversity

*Often God has to shut a door in our face
so that He can subsequently open the door
through which He wants us to go.*

CATHERINE MARSHALL

*Life is literally filled with God-appointed storms.
These squalls surge across everyone's horizon.
We all need them.*

CHARLES SWINDOLL

*Human problems are never greater
than divine solutions.*

ERWIN LUTZER

*God is in control. He may not take away trials or make
detours for us, but He strengthens us through them.*

BILLY GRAHAM

A Timely Tip

When tough times arrive and you're tempted to give in or give up, don't. Instead, work hard and pray harder. Better days may be just around the corner.

5

Anger

A Prayer to Move beyond Angry Feelings

Everyone must be quick to hear, slow to speak,
and slow to anger, for man's anger
does not accomplish God's righteousness.

JAMES 1:19–20 HCSB

Dear Lord, You have warned me that anger is destructive. Yet sometimes I am quick to anger and slow to forgive. Cleanse my heart, Father, of harmful thoughts and hurtful emotions.

I know that You seek the best for me, Lord. And You know that I seek the peace that passes all understanding: Your peace. So give me the wisdom and the strength to turn away from anger.

Help me resist emotional outbursts and refrain from rage.

This day and every day, let me use Jesus as my guide for life, and let me trust His promises now and forever.

Amen

More from God's Word

But I tell you that anyone who is angry with his brother or sister will be subject to judgment.

MATTHEW 5:22 NIV

A hot-tempered man stirs up conflict, but a man slow to anger calms strife.

PROVERBS 15:18 HCSB

Do not let the sun go down on your anger, and do not give the devil an opportunity.

EPHESIANS 4:26–27 NASB

But now you must also put away all the following: anger, wrath, malice, slander, and filthy language from your mouth.

COLOSSIANS 3:8 HCSB

He who is slow to wrath has great understanding, but he who is impulsive exalts folly.

PROVERBS 14:29 NKJV

About Anger

Hot heads and cold hearts never solved anything.

BILLY GRAHAM

*Hence it is not enough to deal with the Temper.
We must go to the source, and change the inmost nature,
and the angry humors will die away of themselves.*

HENRY DRUMMOND

*Anger and bitterness—whatever the cause—
only end up hurting us. Turn that anger over to Christ.*

BILLY GRAHAM

*Frustration is not the will of God. There is time to do
anything and everything that God wants us to do.*

ELISABETH ELLIOT

A Timely Tip

Angry outbursts can be dangerous to your emotional and spiritual health, not to mention your relationships. So treat anger as an uninvited guest, and usher it away as quickly—and as quietly—as possible.

6

Anxiety and Worry

A Prayer to Overcome Worry and Doubt

Cast your burden on the LORD, And He shall sustain you; He shall never permit the righteous to be moved.

PSALM 55:22 NKJV

Dear Lord, You have promised to sustain me in good times and hard times. And, I trust Your promise. But sometimes, I still worry.

When I am tempted to lose faith in the future, give me courage. When my faith begins to waver, help me to trust You more. Then, with Your Holy Word on my lips and with the love of Your Son in my heart, let me live courageously this day and every day.

Keep me mindful, Father, that nothing, absolutely nothing, will happen this day that You and I cannot handle together.

Amen

More from God's Word

Let not your heart be troubled;
you believe in God, believe also in Me.

JOHN 14:1 NKJV

Peace I leave with you; My peace I give to you;
not as the world gives do I give to you.
Do not let your heart be troubled, nor let it be fearful.

JOHN 14:27 NASB

Therefore do not worry about tomorrow,
for tomorrow will worry about its own things.
Sufficient for the day is its own trouble.

MATTHEW 6:34 NKJV

Do not be anxious about anything, but in every
situation, by prayer and petition, with thanksgiving,
present your requests to God.

PHILIPPIANS 4:6 NIV

Cast all your anxiety on him because he cares for you.

I PETER 5:7 NIV

About Anxiety and Worry

Worry is the senseless process
of cluttering up tomorrow's
opportunities with leftover
problems from today.

BARBARA JOHNSON

Pray, and let God worry.

MARTIN LUTHER

Tomorrow is busy
worrying about itself;
don't get tangled up
in its worry-webs.

SARAH YOUNG

A Timely Tip

You have worries, but God has solutions. Your challenge is to trust Him to solve the problems that are simply too big for you to resolve on your own.

7

Asking God

Praying for the Things I Need

*Ask, and it will be given to you; seek,
and you will find; knock, and it will be opened to you.
For everyone who asks receives, and he who
seeks finds, and to him who knocks it will be opened.*

<small>MATTHEW 7:7–8 NASB</small>

Dear Lord, You have promised to hear my requests, and You have promised to answer them in Your own time and in Your own way. For these things, I am profoundly grateful.

Today, Father, I will ask You for the things I need. In every situation, I will come to You in prayer. You know what I want, Lord, and more importantly, You know what I need.

When I have questions, concerns, or fears, I will turn to You, and I will trust Your answers, today, tomorrow, and forever.

Amen

More from God's Word

Until now you have asked for nothing in My name.
Ask and you will receive,
so that your joy may be complete.

JOHN 16:24 HCSB

The effective prayer of a righteous man
can accomplish much.

JAMES 5:16 NASB

You did not choose me, but I chose you
and appointed you to go and bear fruit—
fruit that will last—and so that whatever you ask
in my name the Father will give you.

JOHN 15:16 NIV

Your Father knows the things
you have need of before you ask Him.

MATTHEW 6:8 NKJV

Do not be anxious about anything,
but in every situation, by prayer and petition,
with thanksgiving, present your requests to God.

PHILIPPIANS 4:6 NIV

Asking God for the Things We Need

*It's important that you keep asking God
to show you what He wants you to do.
If you don't ask, you won't know.*

STORMIE OMARTIAN

*We honor God by asking for great things
when they are a part of His promise. We dishonor
Him and cheat ourselves when we ask for molehills
where He has promised mountains.*

VANCE HAVNER

*Are you serious about wanting God's guidance
to become a personal reality in your life?
The first step is to tell God that you know you can't
manage your own life; that you need his help.*

CATHERINE MARSHALL

A Timely Tip

If you want more from life, ask more from God. If you're pursuing a worthy goal, ask for God's help—and keep asking—until He answers your prayers.

8

Attitude

A Prayer for the Right Attitude

Rejoice always; pray without ceasing.

I Thessalonians 5:16–17 NASB

Dear Lord, You have promised that You have prepared a place for me in heaven, and that Your Son came to this world so that I might have a life of spiritual abundance. How richly I am blessed.

Today, Father, I pray for an attitude that is pleasing to You. In every circumstance, I will strive to celebrate the gifts You have given me. I will honor You with my words and deeds, and I will praise You for Your priceless blessings.

Amen

More from God's Word

*Be glad and rejoice, because your
reward is great in heaven.*

MATTHEW 5:12 HCSB

A merry heart makes a cheerful countenance . . .

PROVERBS 15:13 NKJV

*This is the day the LORD has made;
let us rejoice and be glad in it.*

PSALM 118:24 HCSB

*Finally, brothers, rejoice. Become mature,
be encouraged, be of the same mind, be at peace,
and the God of love and peace will be with you.*

II CORINTHIANS 13:11 HCSB

*You must have the same attitude
that Christ Jesus had.*

PHILIPPIANS 2:5 NLT

About Attitude

*Developing a positive attitude means working
continually to find what is uplifting and encouraging.*

BARBARA JOHNSON

*The longer I live, the more convinced I become
that life is 10 percent what happens to us
and 90 percent how we respond to it.*

CHARLES SWINDOLL

*The things we think are the things
that feed our souls. If we think on pure and lovely
things, we shall grow pure and lovely like them;
and the converse is equally true.*

HANNAH WHITALL SMITH

A Timely Tip

As a Christian, you have every reason on earth—
and in heaven—to have a positive attitude. After all,
God's in charge, He loves you, and He's prepared a
place for you to live eternally with Him. And that's
what really matters.

9

Beginnings

A Prayer for New Beginnings

Do not remember the former things, nor consider the things of old. Behold, I will do a new thing.

ISAIAH 43:18–19 NKJV

Dear Lord, You have promised that You have a plan, a perfect plan, for my life. And I know that You have a purpose for me that will bring earthly abundance and eternal joy.

All things are possible for You, Father. You can always renew my strength and restore my spirits. You can transform me, Father, and give me a fresh start, a new beginning.

As I plan for the next stage of my life, I will seek Your guidance and entrust my future to You. I know that You will lead me, Lord, today, tomorrow, and forever.

Amen

More from God's Word

Your old sinful self has died,
and your new life is kept with Christ in God.

Colossians 3:3 NCV

But there is one thing I always do.
Forgetting the past and straining toward
what is ahead, I keep trying to reach the goal
and get the prize for which God called me . . .

Philippians 3:13–14 NCV

"For I know the plans I have for you"—[this is]
the Lord's declaration—"plans for [your] welfare,
not for disaster, to give you a future and a hope."

Jeremiah 29:11 HCSB

Then the One seated on the throne said,
"Look! I am making everything new."

Revelation 21:5 HCSB

You are being renewed in the spirit of your minds;
you put on the new self, the one created according to
God's likeness in righteousness and purity of the truth.

Ephesians 4:23–24 HCSB

About New Beginnings

God specializes in giving people a fresh start.

RICK WARREN

Are you in earnest? Seize this very minute.
What you can do, or dream you can, begin it.
Boldness has genius, power, and magic in it.

JOHANN WOLFGANG VON GOETHE

The best preparation for the future is the present
well seen to, and the last duty done.

GEORGE MACDONALD

Each day you must say to yourself,
"Today I am going to begin."

JEAN PIERRE DE CAUSSADE

A Timely Tip

If you're graduating into a new phase of life, be sure to make God your partner. If you do, He'll guide your steps; He'll help carry your burdens; and He'll help you focus on the things that really matter.

10

Blessings

A Prayer of Gratitude for God's Blessings

May Yahweh bless you and protect you; may Yahweh make His face shine on you and be gracious to you.

Numbers 6:24–25 HCSB

Dear Lord, You have promised to bless me, now and forever. I thank You, Father, for Your gifts, for Your love, and for Your Son.

You have given me so much, Father, and I am eternally grateful. I will spend all eternity praising You.

I know, Lord, that You are the Giver of all good gifts. And I know that every good gift You give me is meant to be shared with others. Today, let me share Your blessings with others, just as You first shared them with me.

Amen

More from God's Word

You will show me the path of life;
in Your presence is fullness of joy;
at Your right hand are pleasures forevermore.

PSALM 16:11 NKJV

The LORD is my rock, my fortress, and my deliverer,
my God, my mountain where I seek refuge.
My shield, the horn of my salvation,
my stronghold, my refuge, and my Savior.

II SAMUEL 22:2–3 HCSB

Blessings crown the head of the righteous . . .

PROVERBS 10:6 NIV

The LORD is my shepherd; I shall not want.

PSALM 23:1 KJV

The LORD is good to all:
and his tender mercies are over all his works.

PSALM 145:9 KJV

About God's Blessings

God is the giver,
and we are the receivers.
And His richest gifts are bestowed
not upon those who do
the greatest things, but upon
those who accept His abundance
and His grace.

HANNAH WHITALL SMITH

God is always trying to give
good things to us,
but our hands are
too full to receive them.

ST. AUGUSTINE

God's gifts put man's best dreams to shame.

ELIZABETH BARRETT BROWNING

A Timely Tip

God has given you more blessings than you can possibly count, but it doesn't hurt to begin counting them. And while you're at it, don't forget to praise the Giver of these incalculable gifts.

11

Busyness

A Prayer for Busy Times

Return unto thy rest, O my soul;
for the LORD hath dealt bountifully with thee.

PSALM 116:7 KJV

Heavenly Father, sometimes I am distracted by the complications of the day or by the demands of the moment. When I am worried or fretful, Father, let me turn my thoughts back to You.

You offer me peace, Lord, a peace that the world can never give. Today, I will open my heart to You and accept the peace that passes all understanding: Your peace. And I will strive to follow in the footsteps of Your Son, today, tomorrow, and forever.

Amen

More from God's Word

*Come unto me, all ye that labour
and are heavy laden, and I will give you rest.*

MATTHEW 11:28 KJV

*Be still before the LORD
and wait patiently for Him.*

PSALM 37:7 NIV

*And the peace of God, which surpasses
all comprehension, will guard your hearts
and your minds in Christ Jesus.*

PHILIPPIANS 4:7 NASB

*Rest in God alone, my soul,
for my hope comes from Him.*

PSALM 62:5 HCSB

*In quietness and in confidence
shall be your strength.*

ISAIAH 30:15 KJV

About Busyness

Prescription for a happier and healthier life:
resolve to slow your pace; learn to say no gracefully;
reject the temptation to chase after more pleasures,
more hobbies, and more social entanglements.

JAMES DOBSON

We hurt people by being too busy.
Too busy to notice their needs. Too busy to listen
when someone needs to talk. Too busy to care.

BILLY GRAHAM

If you refuse to be hurried and pressed,
if you stay your soul on God, nothing can keep you
from that clearness of spirit which is life and peace.
In that stillness you know what His will is.

AMY CARMICHAEL

A Timely Tip

The world, which is filled with temptations and distractions, wants to grab every minute of your time, but God wants your attention too. When in doubt, trust God.

12

Celebration

A Prayer of Celebration

Rejoice in the Lord always. Again I will say, rejoice!

PHILIPPIANS 4:4 NKJV

Heavenly Father, Your Word promises that this day, like every other day, is a cause for celebration. So today, I will celebrate my life.

I will count my blessings, not my hardships. I will look for the good in all people. I will rejoice in tasks you have given me, and I will celebrate the lives of my friends and family.

Thank You, Lord, for Your love. Let me treasure Your blessings—and share them—this day and forevermore.

Amen

More from God's Word

A happy heart is like a continual feast.

PROVERBS 15:15 NCV

Rejoice always, pray without ceasing,
in everything give thanks;
for this is the will of God
in Christ Jesus for you.

I THESSALONIANS 5:16–18 NKJV

I came that they may have life,
and have it abundantly.

JOHN 10:10 NASB

I delight greatly in the LORD;
my soul rejoices in my God.

ISAIAH 61:10 NIV

This is the day which the LORD has made;
let us rejoice and be glad in it.

PSALM 118:24 NASB

About Celebration

*Every day we live is a priceless gift of God,
loaded with possibilities to learn something new,
to gain fresh insights.*

DALE EVANS ROGERS

*The greatest honor you can give Almighty God
is to live gladly and joyfully because
of the knowledge of His love.*

JULIANA OF NORWICH

*All our life is celebration to us. We are convinced,
in fact, that God is always everywhere.*

ST. CLEMENT OF ALEXANDRIA

*There is not one blade of grass, there is no color
in this world that is not intended to make men rejoice.*

JOHN CALVIN

A Timely Tip

Every day is a glorious opportunity to celebrate life
by loving your neighbor and serving your Creator. Join
the celebration.

13

Charity and Generosity

Praying for a Generous Heart

So let each one give as he purposes
in his heart, not grudgingly or of necessity;
for God loves a cheerful giver.

II CORINTHIANS 9:7 NKJV

Dear Lord, You have promised that You love a cheerful giver. And your Word teaches me that it is more blessed to give than to receive. Make me a faithful steward of Your gifts and let me share those gifts with others, today and every day that I live.

Make me a generous and cheerful giver, Father, so that my actions might be pleasing to You. So today, I will give generously of my time and my possessions as I care for those in need.

And as I serve Your children, make me a humble giver, Lord, so that all the praise and the glory might be Yours.

Amen

More from God's Word

Freely you have received; freely give.

MATTHEW 10:8 NIV

If you have two shirts, give one to the poor.
If you have food, share it with those who are hungry.

LUKE 3:11 NLT

Truly I tell you, whatever you did for one of the least
of these brothers and sisters of mine, you did for me.

MATTHEW 25:40 NIV

Therefore, whenever we have the opportunity,
we should do good to everyone,
especially to those in the family of faith.

GALATIANS 6:10 NLT

You should remember the words of the Lord Jesus:
"It is more blessed to give than to receive."

ACTS 20:35 NLT

About Charity and Generosity

*The goodness you receive from God
is a treasure for you to share with others.*

ELIZABETH GEORGE

*In Jesus the service of God and the service
of the least of the brethren were one.*

DIETRICH BONHOEFFER

*A cheerful giver does not count the cost
of what he gives. His heart is set on pleasing
and cheering him to whom the gift is given.*

JULIANA OF NORWICH

Christian life consists in faith and charity.

MARTIN LUTHER

A Timely Tip

There's a direct relationship between generosity and joy—the more you share with others, the more joy you'll experience for yourself.

14

Cheerfulness

Praying for a Cheerful Heart

A cheerful heart has a continual feast.

<small>PROVERBS 15:15 HCSB</small>

Heavenly Father, Your Word promises that a cheerful heart is a source of great joy and comfort. Make me a cheerful Christian, today and every day of my life.

You have blessed me so richly, Father, that I have every reason to celebrate my life. And You have given me so many reasons to rejoice. For these gifts, I praise You.

Today, I will choose an attitude of cheerfulness. I will strive to be a joyful believer, Lord, quick to smile and slow to anger.

Amen

More from God's Word

*Rejoice always, pray without ceasing,
in everything give thanks; for this is the will
of God in Christ Jesus for you.*

I THESSALONIANS 5:16–18 NKJV

*Shout for joy to the LORD, all the earth.
Worship the LORD with gladness;
come before him with joyful songs.*

PSALM 100:1–2 NIV

*A cheerful heart is good medicine,
but a crushed spirit dries up the bones.*

PROVERBS 17:22 NIV

*Do everything without grumbling and arguing,
so that you may be blameless and pure.*

PHILIPPIANS 2:14–15 HCSB

*This is the day that the LORD has made.
Let us rejoice and be glad today!*

PSALM 118:24 NCV

About Cheerfulness

The greatest honor you
can give Almighty God
is to live gladly and joyfully
because of the knowledge of His love.

JULIANA OF NORWICH

The practical effect
of Christianity is happiness,
therefore let it be spread
abroad everywhere!

C. H. SPURGEON

A life of intimacy with God
is characterized by joy.

OSWALD CHAMBERS

A Timely Tip

Cheerfulness is its own reward, but not its only reward. When you sow a positive attitude, you'll reap a positive life.

15

Christ's Love

A Prayer of Gratitude for Christ's Love

As the Father loved Me,
I also have loved you; abide in My love.

JOHN 15:9 NKJV

Heavenly Father, Your Word promises that Jesus died so that I can live eternally with You. I am humbled by Christ's love and by His sacrifice.

Thank You, Father, for Your Son, and for the priceless gift of eternal life. You loved me first, Lord, and I will return Your love, today and forever.

I praise You, Father, for a love that never ends. I will return Your love and share it with the world.

Amen

More from God's Word

*I am the good shepherd. The good shepherd
lays down his life for the sheep.*

John 10:11 HCSB

*For Christ also suffered once for sins,
the just for the unjust, that He might bring
us to God, being put to death in the flesh
but made alive by the Spirit.*

I Peter 3:18 NKJV

*For God so loved the world, that he gave
his only begotten Son, that whosoever believeth
in him should not perish, but have everlasting life.*

John 3:16 KJV

We love him, because he first loved us.

I John 4:19 KJV

*No one has greater love than this,
that someone would lay down his life for his friends.*

John 15:13 HCSB

About Christ's Love

Jesus is all compassion.
He never betrays us.

CATHERINE MARSHALL

The love of God exists in its strongest
and purest form in the very midst
of suffering and tragedy.

SUZANNE DALE EZELL

As the love of a husband for his bride,
such is the love of Christ for His people.

C. H. SPURGEON

Jesus: the proof of God's love.

PHILIP YANCEY

A Timely Tip

Christ's love is meant to be experienced—and shared—by you.

16

Circumstances

A Prayer for Difficult Circumstances

Trust in him at all times, O people; pour out your hearts to him, for God is our refuge.

<small>PSALM 62:8 NIV</small>

Dear Lord, when my life seems to be spinning out of control, give me the wisdom to turn everything over to You. Keep me mindful that You are always with me and that no problem is too big for You.

Whatever my circumstances, I will trust You. In good times and hard times, I will praise You, Father, knowing that You understand the wisdom of Your perfect plan.

I know that every day is a gift, Lord. And this is the day that You have made. I will rejoice and be glad in it.

Amen

More from God's Word

The LORD is a refuge for His people
and a stronghold . . .

JOEL 3:16 NASB

Cast your burden on the LORD,
And He shall sustain you;
He shall never permit the righteous to be moved.

PSALM 55:22 NKJV

I have learned in whatever state I am,
to be content.

PHILIPPIANS 4:11 NKJV

God is our protection and our strength.
He always helps in times of trouble.

PSALM 46:1 NCV

The LORD is a refuge for the oppressed,
a refuge in times of trouble.

PSALM 9:9 HCSB

About Difficult Circumstances

*Don't let obstacles along the road to eternity
shake your confidence in God's promises.*

DAVID JEREMIAH

*No matter what our circumstance,
we can find a reason to be thankful.*

DAVID JEREMIAH

*Accept each day as it comes to you.
Do not waste your time and energy
wishing for a different set of circumstances.*

SARAH YOUNG

*Every experience God gives us, every person
He brings into our lives, is the perfect preparation
for the future that only He can see.*

CORRIE TEN BOOM

A Timely Tip

A change of circumstances is rarely as important as a change in attitude. If you change your thoughts, you will most certainly change your circumstances.

17

Comforting Others

Praying for Those Who Need Comfort

Therefore, God's chosen ones, holy and loved,
put on heartfelt compassion, kindness,
humility, gentleness, and patience.

<small>COLOSSIANS 3:12 HCSB</small>

Dear Lord, this world can be a difficult place. And so many people are suffering. Let me be a beacon of encouragement to those who have lost hope.

Let me comfort those who grieve. Help me help the helpless and lift up the downtrodden. Let me offer kind words and good deeds to the people I meet along the way. And let me share Your love and spread Your Word to a world that needs both.

So many people in this world have so many needs. Let me be quick to help and quick to offer comfort, while there's still time.

Amen

More from God's Word

Let us think about each other and help each other
to show love and do good deeds.

HEBREWS 10:24 NCV

Do to others as you would have them do to you.

LUKE 6:31 NIV

Carry one another's burdens;
in this way you will fulfill the law of Christ.

GALATIANS 6:2 HCSB

So let's not get tired of doing what is good.
At just the right time we will reap a harvest
of blessing if we don't give up.

GALATIANS 6:9 NLT

Do not withhold good from those to whom it is due,
when it is in your power to act.

PROVERBS 3:27 NIV

Comforting Others

God doesn't comfort us to make us comfortable,
but to make us comforters.

BILLY GRAHAM

A Christian is someone who shares
the sufferings of God in the world.

DIETRICH BONHOEFFER

Jesus went without comfort so that you might have it.
He postponed joy so that you might share in it.

JONI EARECKSON TADA

When we are the comfort and encouragement
to others, we are sometimes surprised
at how it comes back to us many times over.

BILLY GRAHAM

A Timely Tip

Today, you'll encounter someone who needs your encouragement and your comfort. When it happens, God wants you to share His message and His love.

18

Confidence

A Prayer for Confidence

*So we may boldly say: "The Lord is my helper;
I will not fear. What can man do to me?"*

<small>HEBREWS 13:6 NKJV</small>

Heavenly Father, you have promised to be my protector and my helper. Because I trust Your promises, Lord, I have nothing to fear.

When I place my confidence in the material world, I will inevitably be disappointed. But when I put my confidence in You, I am secure.

Dear Lord, give me confidence and courage for the day ahead. When I am fearful, let me feel Your strength. Let me gain confidence from Your promises and from Your unending love, now and forever.

Amen

More from God's Word

You are my hope; O LORD God,
You are my confidence.

PSALM 71:5 NASB

God is our refuge and strength,
a very present help in trouble.

PSALM 46:1 NKJV

In this world you will have trouble.
But take heart! I have overcome the world.

JOHN 16:33 NIV

Be strong and courageous, and do the work.
Don't be afraid or discouraged,
for the LORD God, my God, is with you.
He won't leave you or forsake you . . .

I CHRONICLES 28:20 HCSB

I lift up my eyes to the hills—
where does my help come from?
My help comes from the LORD,
the Maker of heaven and earth.

PSALM 121:1–2 NIV

About Confidence

You need to make the right decision—
firmly and decisively—and then stick with it,
with God's help.

BILLY GRAHAM

We never get anywhere—
nor do our conditions and circumstances change—
when we look at the dark side of life.

LETTIE COWMAN

Confidence in the natural world is self-reliance;
in the spiritual world, it is God-reliance.

OSWALD CHAMBERS

Never yield to gloomy anticipation.

LETTIE COWMAN

A Timely Tip

As a Christian, you have every reason to be confident. With God as your partner, you have nothing to fear.

19

Contentment

Praying for a Contented Heart

I have learned in whatever state I am, to be content.

PHILIPPIANS 4:11 NKJV

Heavenly Father, Your promises offer me contentment and peace. Help me to trust Your Word, to follow Your commandments, and to welcome the peace of Jesus into my heart.

When I turn my thoughts and prayers to You, I feel the peace and fulfillment that You intend for my life. You give me peace when I draw close to You. I will honor You with my prayers and my service.

Let me trust Your will and accept Your peace, Dear Lord, today, tomorrow, and forever.

Amen

More from God's Word

But godliness with contentment is a great gain.
I TIMOTHY 6:6 HCSB

A tranquil heart is life to the body,
but jealousy is rottenness to the bones.
PROVERBS 14:30 HCSB

The peace of God, which passeth
all understanding, shall keep your hearts
and minds through Christ Jesus.
PHILIPPIANS 4:7 KJV

Come unto me, all ye that labour
and are heavy laden, and I will give you rest.
MATTHEW 11:28 KJV

Make sure that your character is free from the love
of money, being content with what you have;
for He Himself has said, "I WILL NEVER DESERT YOU,
NOR WILL I EVER FORSAKE YOU."

HEBREWS 13:5 NASB

About Contentment

Those who are God's without reserve are,
in every sense, content.

HANNAH WHITALL SMITH

Contentment is possible when
we stop striving for more.

CHARLES SWINDOLL

When you truly know God,
you have energy to serve him,
boldness to share him, and contentment in him.

J. I. PACKER

No matter what you're facing, embrace life in trust
and contentment based on your faith in Jesus.

ELIZABETH GEORGE

A Timely Tip

Contentment comes, not from your circumstances, but from your attitude and your faith. So stay positive and remember that faith is the foundation of a contented life.

20

Courage

A Prayer for Courage

Be strong and courageous, and do the work.
Do not be afraid or discouraged,
for the LORD God, my God, is with you.

I CHRONICLES 28:20 NIV

Dear Lord, today I ask You for courage. I ask that you give me the wisdom to know what's right and the strength to do what's right.

Sometimes, I face difficulties that almost overwhelm me, and I am tempted to give up. But I know that you are always with me, Father, always ready to guide me and protect me. So I can take comfort that You have promised to be my shepherd, today and forever.

This is the day that You have made, Lord, and I will use it wisely. I ask that You lead me on the proper path—Your path—and that You give me the courage to do what's right, even when it's hard.

Amen

More from God's Word

Be on guard. Stand true to what you believe.
Be courageous. Be strong.

I Corinthians 16:13 NLT

I can do all things through Him
who strengthens me.

Philippians 4:13 NASB

Behold, God is my salvation;
I will trust, and not be afraid . . .

Isaiah 12:2 KJV

But He said to them,
"It is I; do not be afraid."

John 6:20 NKJV

For God has not given us a spirit of fearfulness,
but one of power, love, and sound judgment.

II Timothy 1:7 HCSB

About Courage

Courage is not simply one of the virtues,
but the form of every virtue at the testing point.

C. S. LEWIS

Do not limit the limitless God! With Him,
face the future unafraid because you are never alone.

LETTIE COWMAN

In my experience, God rarely makes
our fear disappear. Instead,
He asks us to be strong and take courage.

BRUCE WILKINSON

Just as courage is faith in good, so discouragement
is faith in evil, and, while courage opens
the door to good, discouragement opens it to evil.

HANNAH WHITALL SMITH

A Timely Tip

If your courage is being tested today, hold fast to God's promises and pray. God will give you the strength to meet any challenge if you ask Him sincerely and often. So ask.

21

Decisions

Praying for Wise Decisions

But if any of you needs wisdom, you should ask God for it. He is generous and enjoys giving to everyone and will give you wisdom without criticizing you.

JAMES 1:5 NCV

Heavenly Father, Your Word promises that You will give me the insight to make wise decisions and the courage to act upon the decisions that I make. I thank You for Your guidance, Lord.

Today, I ask You to guide me along a path of Your choosing. Help me to make decisions that are pleasing to You. Help me to be honest, patient, and obedient. And above all, help me to follow the teachings of Your Son, not just today, but every day.

Dear Father, I will focus my thoughts on Your will for my life. I will strive to make decisions that are pleasing to You, and I will strive to follow in the footsteps of Your Son.

Amen

More from God's Word

In every way be an example of doing good deeds.
When you teach, do it with honesty and seriousness.

TITUS 2:7 NCV

Blessed is the man who walks not in the counsel
of the ungodly, nor stands in the path of sinners,
nor sits in the seat of the scornful.

PSALM 1:1 NKJV

Wherefore by their fruits ye shall know them.

MATTHEW 7:20 KJV

The highway of the upright avoids evil;
the one who guards his way protects his life.

PROVERBS 16:17 HCSB

We can gather our thoughts, but the LORD gives
the right answer. People may be pure in their own eyes,
but the LORD examines their motives.

PROVERBS 16:1–2 NLT

About Making Decisions

*A man who honors God privately will
show it by making good decisions publicly.*

EDWIN LOUIS COLE

*Your choices and decisions are a reflection of how
well you've set and followed your priorities.*

ELIZABETH GEORGE

*Get into the habit of dealing with
God about everything.*

OSWALD CHAMBERS

*Every day, I find countless opportunities to decide
whether I will obey God and demonstrate my love
for Him or try to please myself or the world system.
God is waiting for my choices.*

BILL BRIGHT

A Timely Tip

Every step of your life's journey is a choice, and the
overall quality of your decisions will help determine
the overall quality of the journey.

22

Disappointments

Moving Past the Disappointments

*Then they cried out to the LORD in their trouble,
and He saved them out of their distresses.*

PSALM 107:13 NKJV

Dear Lord, You have promised to love and protect me, as a shepherd watches over his flock. I trust Your promise, Father. Your assurance gives me comfort in good times and hard times.

When I suffer the inevitable setbacks of life, the Bible reminds me that You are in control. You are the Giver of all good things, Father. I am blessed by Your grace.

Wherever I find myself, whether on the mountaintops of life or in the valleys, I will celebrate more and worry less. When my faith begins to waver, I will trust You more. Then, with praise on my lips and love in my heart, I will live courageously, faithfully, and thankfully.

Amen

More from God's Word

He heals the brokenhearted
and binds up their wounds.

PSALM 147:3 HCSB

Many adversities come to the one
who is righteous, but the LORD
delivers him from them all.

PSALM 34:19 HCSB

They that sow in tears shall reap in joy.

PSALM 126:5 KJV

My son, do not despise the chastening of the Lord,
nor be discouraged when you are rebuked by Him.

HEBREWS 12:5 NKJV

He shall not be afraid of evil tidings:
his heart is fixed, trusting in the LORD.

PSALM 112:7 KJV

About Life's Inevitable Disappointments

We all have sorrows and disappointments,
but one must never forget that, if commended to God,
they will issue in good. His own solution
is far better than any we could conceive.

FANNY CROSBY

Discouragement is the opposite of faith. It is Satan's
device to thwart the work of God in your life.

BILLY GRAHAM

If your hopes are being disappointed just now,
it means that they are being purified.

OSWALD CHAMBERS

Unless we learn to deal with disappointment,
it will rob us of joy and poison our souls.

BILLY GRAHAM

A Timely Tip

When you're discouraged, disappointed, or hurt,
don't spend too much time asking, "Why me, Lord?"
Instead, ask, "What now, Lord?" and then get busy.
When you do, you'll feel much better.

23

Dreams

Big Dreams

Hope deferred makes the heart sick,
but a dream fulfilled is a tree of life.

PROVERBS 13:12 NLT

Dear Lord, You have promised that all things are possible through You. And I trust that promise. Because You are my Father, I have the courage to make big plans and the determination to pursue my dreams.

When I am weary, worried, or confused, You give me strength. When I am discouraged, You restore my spirit. When I am fearful, Your Word teaches me to rely on You.

Today, keep me mindful of Your healing power and Your infinite love. And let me dream big dreams. Because all things are possible through You.

Amen

More from God's Word

Hope deferred makes the heart sick.

PROVERBS 13:12 NKJV

*But we are hoping for something we do not have yet,
and we are waiting for it patiently.*

ROMANS 8:25 NCV

*Humble yourselves therefore under the mighty hand
of God, that he may exalt you in due time.*

I PETER 5:6 KJV

*Now may the God of hope fill you with all joy and
peace as you believe in Him so that you may overflow
with hope by the power of the Holy Spirit.*

ROMANS 15:13 HCSB

Where there is no vision, the people perish . . .

PROVERBS 29:18 KJV

About Dreams

Allow your dreams a place in your prayers and plans.
God-given dreams can help you move into the future
He is preparing for you.

BARBARA JOHNSON

God's gifts put man's best dreams to shame.

ELIZABETH BARRETT BROWNING

When the dream of our heart is one that God
has planted there, a strange happiness flows into us.
At that moment, the spiritual resources
of the universe are released to help us.

CATHERINE MARSHALL

A Timely Tip

You can dream big dreams, but you can never out-dream God. His plans for you are even bigger than you can imagine. Entrust your future to Him.

24

Enthusiasm

Praying for Enthusiasm

Whatever you do, do it enthusiastically,
as something done for the Lord and not for men.

<small>COLOSSIANS 3:23 HCSB</small>

Heavenly Father, Your Word promises that nothing is impossible for You. Your power, like Your love, is infinite. Because You love me, I can celebrate my life here on earth and my eternal life with You.

This Christian life is an amazing adventure. Because of Your grace, I have every reason on earth—and in heaven—to share my joy and my enthusiasm with a world that needs both.

So let me be an enthusiastic believer, Lord, and let me share my enthusiasm with others. So many people need to hear the good news of Your Son. Let me share His story enthusiastically and often.

Amen

More from God's Word

Do your work with enthusiasm.
Work as if you were serving the Lord,
not as if you were serving only men and women.

Ephesians 6:7 NCV

But as for me, I will hope continually,
and will praise You yet more and more.

Psalm 71:14 NASB

Let the hearts of those who seek the Lord rejoice.
Look to the Lord and his strength; seek his face always.

I Chronicles 16:10–11 NIV

Rejoice always! Pray constantly.
Give thanks in everything,
for this is God's will for you in Christ Jesus.

I Thessalonians 5:16–18 HCSB

A happy heart makes the face cheerful,
but heartache crushes the spirit.

Proverbs 15:13 NIV

About Enthusiasm

*Joy comes not from what
we have but what we are.*

C. H. SPURGEON

*Developing a positive attitude means
working continually to find
what is uplifting and encouraging.*

BARBARA JOHNSON

*Wherever you are, be all there!
Live to the hilt every situation
you believe to be the will of God.*

JIM ELLIOT

A Timely Tip

Look upon your life as an exciting adventure because that's precisely what it can be—and should be.

25

Eternal Life

Gratitude for the
Gift of Eternal Life

*For God so loved the world, that he gave his only
begotten Son, that whosoever believeth in him
should not perish, but have everlasting life.*

JOHN 3:16 KJV

Heavenly Father, You have offered me the gift of
eternal life through Your Son. I accept Your gift, Lord,
with praise and thanksgiving.

Jesus made the ultimate sacrifice on the cross. He
gave His earthly life so that I might live with Him in
heaven. Let me share the good news of my salvation
with those who need Christ's healing touch.

Dear Lord, keep the hope of heaven fresh in my
heart. And while I am in this world, help me pass
through it with faith in my heart and praise on my lips
for You.

Amen

More from God's Word

I assure you: Anyone who hears My word and believes Him who sent Me has eternal life and will not come under judgment, but has passed from death to life.

JOHN 5:24 HCSB

I have written these things to you who believe in the name of the Son of God, so that you may know that you have eternal life.

I JOHN 5:13 HCSB

The last enemy that will be destroyed is death.

I CORINTHIANS 15:26 NKJV

The world and its desires pass away, but the man who does the will of God lives forever.

I JOHN 2:17 NIV

For the wages of sin is death, but the gift of God is eternal life in Christ Jesus our Lord.

ROMANS 6:23 NIV

About Eternal Life

Death is not the end of life;
it is only the gateway to eternity.

BILLY GRAHAM

No matter what our circumstance,
we can find a reason to be thankful.

DAVID JEREMIAH

Everything that is joined to the immortal head
will share His immortality.

C. S. LEWIS

Death is not a journeying into an unknown land. It is
a voyage home. We are not going to a strange country
but to our Father's house, and among our kith and kin.

JOHN RUSKIN

A Timely Tip

God offers you the priceless gift of eternal life. If you have not accepted His gift, the appropriate moment to do so is now.

26

Faith

A Prayer for Faith

For truly I say to you, if you have faith the size
of a mustard seed, you shall say to this mountain,
"Move from here to there," and it will move;
and nothing shall be impossible to you.

<small>MATTHEW 17:20 NASB</small>

Heavenly Father, You have promised that with faith, I can move the mountains in my life. As I take the next steps on my life's journey, I will take those steps with You.

Because of my faith in You, I can be courageous and strong. I will lean upon You, Father—and trust you—now and forever.

Lord, let me remember that You are always near and that You can overcome any challenge. Keep me mindful of Your love and Your power, so I can live fearlessly and faithfully, today and every day.

Amen

More from God's Word

Don't be afraid, because I am your God.
I will make you strong and will help you;
I will support you with my right hand that saves you.

ISAIAH 41:10 NCV

Blessed are they that have not seen,
and yet have believed.

JOHN 20:29 KJV

And he said unto her, Daughter,
thy faith hath made thee whole;
go in peace, and be whole . . .

MARK 5:34 KJV

All things are possible
for the one who believes.

MARK 9:23 NCV

Don't be afraid. Only believe.

MARK 5:36 HCSB

About Faith

Shout the shout of faith. Nothing can withstand the triumphant faith that links itself to omnipotence. The secret of all successful living lies in this shout of faith.

HANNAH WHITALL SMITH

Faith points us beyond our problems to the hope we have in Christ.

BILLY GRAHAM

Faith is not merely holding on to God. It is God holding on to you.

CORRIE TEN BOOM

Faith does not concern itself with the entire journey. One step is enough.

LETTIE COWMAN

A Timely Tip

If your faith is strong enough, you and God—working together—can move mountains. No challenge is too big for God.

27

Family

A Prayer for My Family

*Choose for yourselves this day whom
you will serve . . . . But as for me and my house,
we will serve the LORD.*

JOSHUA 24:15 NKJV

Dear Heavenly Father, You have blessed me with a
family to love and to care for. Protect my family, Lord.
And let me show them love and acceptance, so that
through me they might come to know You.

Lord, you have promised that love never ends. I
thank You for loved ones who are quick to pray for me.
Let me be quick to pray for them. And let me demonstrate my love by the things that I say and the things
that I do, today and every day of my life.

Amen

More from God's Word

Every kingdom divided against itself is headed for destruction, and a house divided against itself falls.

LUKE 11:17 HCSB

Better a dry crust with peace than a house full of feasting with strife.

PROVERBS 17:1 HCSB

But now faith, hope, love, abide these three; but the greatest of these is love.

I CORINTHIANS 13:13 NASB

Their first responsibility is to show godliness at home and repay their parents by taking care of them. This is something that pleases God very much.

I TIMOTHY 5:4 NLT

But if anyone does not provide for his own, and especially for those of his household, he has denied the faith and is worse than an unbeliever.

I TIMOTHY 5:8 NASB

About Family

Faith in Christ is the most important of all principles in building a happy marriage and a successful home.

BILLY GRAHAM

I like to think of my family as a big, beautiful patchwork quilt—each of us so different yet stitched together by love and life experiences.

BARBARA JOHNSON

Line by line, moment by moment, special times are etched into our memories in the permanent ink of everlasting love in our relationships.

GLORIA GAITHER

A family is a place where principles are hammered out and honed on the anvil of everyday living.

CHARLES SWINDOLL

A Timely Tip

Your family is a precious gift from above, a gift that should be treasured, nurtured, protected, and loved.

28

Fear

Freedom from Fear

*Even though I walk through the valley of the shadow
of death, I will fear no evil, for you are with me;
your rod and your staff, they comfort me.*

PSALM 23:4 NIV

Dear Lord, You have promised that even when I walk
through the valley of the shadow of death, You are with
me. And I trust Your promise. Thank You, Father, for
Your perfect love, a love that casts out fear and gives
me the courage to meet the challenges of this world.

Heavenly Father, when I am anxious, keep me
mindful that You are my shepherd. When I am weary,
give me strength. Give me the confidence, Father, to
face the challenges of this day as I gain my courage
from You. With You as my protector, I have nothing
to fear.

Amen

More from God's Word

But He said to them, "It is I; do not be afraid."
JOHN 6:20 NKJV

The LORD is my light and my salvation—
whom should I fear? The Lord is the stronghold
of my life—of whom should I be afraid?
PSALM 27:1 HCSB

Be not afraid, only believe.
MARK 5:36 KJV

Peace I leave with you; My peace I give to you;
not as the world gives do I give to you.
Do not let your heart be troubled, nor let it be fearful.
JOHN 14:27 NASB

Fear not, for I am with you; Be not dismayed,
for I am your God. I will strengthen you,
Yes, I will help you, I will uphold you with
My righteous right hand.
ISAIAH 41:10 NKJV

About Fear

The presence of fear
does not mean
you have no faith.
Fear visits everyone.
But make your fear a visitor
and not a resident.

MAX LUCADO

A perfect faith would lift us
absolutely above fear.

GEORGE MACDONALD

It is good to remind ourselves
that the will of God comes from
the heart of God and that
we need not be afraid.

WARREN WIERSBE

A Timely Tip

Everybody faces obstacles. Don't overestimate the size of yours.

29

Following Christ

A Prayer about Discipleship

*Then He said to them all, "If anyone wants
to come with Me, he must deny himself,
take up his cross daily, and follow Me."*

LUKE 9:23 HCSB

Lord Jesus, You have asked me to take up Your cross
and follow You. My life has been changed forever by
Your love and Your sacrifice. Today, I will praise You, I
will honor You, and I will walk with You.

Jesus, I am blessed by Your love. And I am blessed
to be Your disciple. I will trust You, I will obey Your
teachings, and I will share Your good news with the
world, today, tomorrow, and forever.

Amen

More from God's Word

But whoever keeps His word, truly in him
the love of God is perfected. This is how we know
we are in Him: the one who says he remains
in Him should walk just as He walked.

I JOHN 2:5–6 HCSB

For we walk by faith, not by sight.

II CORINTHIANS 5:7 HCSB

Whoever is not willing to carry the cross and follow
me is not worthy of me. Those who try to hold on
to their lives will give up true life. Those who give up
their lives for me will hold on to true life.

MATTHEW 10:38–39 NCV

Take my yoke upon you, and learn of me;
for I am meek and lowly in heart:
and ye shall find rest unto your souls.
For my yoke is easy, and my burden is light.

MATTHEW 11:29–30 KJV

Walk in a manner worthy of the God who
calls you into His own kingdom and glory.

I THESSALONIANS 2:12 NASB

About Following Christ

A disciple is a follower of Christ. That means you take on His priorities as your own. His agenda becomes your agenda. His mission becomes your mission.

CHARLES STANLEY

Choose Jesus Christ! Deny yourself, take up the Cross, and follow Him, for the world must be shown. The world must see, in us, a discernible, visible, startling difference.

ELISABETH ELLIOT

The crucial question for each of us is this: What do you think of Jesus, and do you yet have a personal acquaintance with Him?

HANNAH WHITALL SMITH

Be assured, if you walk with Him and look to Him, and expect help from Him, He will never fail you.

GEORGE MUELLER

A Timely Tip

Every life is built upon something. Let the foundation of your life be the love of God and the salvation of Christ. It's the foundation that cannot be shaken.

30

Forgiveness

Praying for a Forgiving Heart

Judge not, and you shall not be judged.
Condemn not, and you shall not be condemned.
Forgive, and you will be forgiven.

Luke 6:37 NKJV

Dear Lord, You have promised that when I forgive others, I will be forgiven. And I trust Your promise.

Father, You know that an attitude of forgiveness is a priceless gift that I can give to myself. Help me to forgive those who have hurt me, Father, so that I might experience the peace that passes human understanding: Your peace.

When I make mistakes, Lord, You have forgiven me. Let me forgive myself. When I disobey You, give me a repentant heart. And whatever my circumstances, keep me mindful that I am Yours, today, tomorrow, and forever.

Amen

More from God's Word

Above all, love each other deeply,
because love covers a multitude of sins.

I Peter 4:8 NIV

And be kind to one another,
tenderhearted, forgiving one another,
just as God in Christ forgave you.

Ephesians 4:32 NKJV

The merciful are blessed,
for they will be shown mercy.

Matthew 5:7 HCSB

And whenever you stand praying,
if you have anything against anyone,
forgive him, so that your Father in heaven
may also forgive you your wrongdoing.

Mark 11:25 HCSB

But I say to you, love your enemies,
and pray for those who persecute you.

Matthew 5:44 NASB

About Forgiveness

Forgiveness does not change the past,
but it does enlarge the future.

DAVID JEREMIAH

Forgiveness is God's command.

MARTIN LUTHER

Forgiveness is an act of the will,
and the will can function regardless
of the temperature of the heart.

CORRIE TEN BOOM

In one bold stroke, forgiveness obliterates
the past and permits us to enter
the land of new beginnings.

BILLY GRAHAM

A Timely Tip

Forgiveness is its own reward. Bitterness is its own punishment. Guard your words and thoughts accordingly.

31

Friends

Praying for My Friends

A friend loves at all times,
and a brother is born for adversity.

PROVERBS 17:17 NIV

Heavenly Father, You have promised that You seek abundance and joy for me and for all Your children. One way I can share Your joy is through the gift of friendship.

I thank You for my friends, and I pray for them. You have brought wonderful Christian friends into my life. Let our friendships honor You as we walk in the footsteps of Your Son.

Lord, help me to be a loyal friend, ready to listen, ready to encourage, and ready to offer a helping hand. And let the love of Jesus shine through me, today and forever.

Amen

More from God's Word

As iron sharpens iron,
so people can improve each other.

PROVERBS 27:17 NCV

It is good and pleasant when God's people
live together in peace!

PSALM 133:1 NCV

Thine own friend, and thy father's friend,
forsake not . . .

PROVERBS 27:10 KJV

Dear friends, if God loved us in this way,
we also must love one another.

I JOHN 4:11 HCSB

Oil and incense bring joy to the heart,
and the sweetness of a friend is better than self-counsel.

PROVERBS 27:9 HCSB

About Friends

Friendship is one of the sweetest joys of life.
Many might have failed beneath the bitterness
of their trial had they not found a friend.

C. H. Spurgeon

I cannot even imagine where I would be today
were it not for that handful of friends
who have given me a heart full of joy.
Let's face it: friends make life a lot more fun.

Charles Swindoll

A real friend is one who helps us to think our best
thoughts, do our noblest deeds, and be our finest selves.

Elizabeth George

A friend is one who makes me do my best.

Oswald Chambers

A Timely Tip

The best rule for making and keeping friends is, not surprisingly, the Golden one. To have good friends, be a good friend.

32

God First

Putting God First

You shall have no other gods before Me.

Exodus 20:3 NKJV

Heavenly Father, Your Word instructs me to place You first in every aspect of my life. Because I trust Your promises, I understand the need to give you first place in my heart.

The world offers countless temptations and distractions. These worldly priorities sap my energy, monopolize my time, and encourage me to ignore You. I pray for the strength to resist these temptations.

You have blessed me beyond measure, Lord, and I will praise You with my prayers, with my testimony, and with my service, this day and every day. And I will put You first, ahead of every other priority.

Amen

More from God's Word

Therefore, whether you eat or drink,
or whatever you do, do all to the glory of God.

I Corinthians 10:31 NKJV

How happy is everyone who fears the Lord,
who walks in His ways!

Psalm 128:1 HCSB

We love him, because he first loved us.

I John 4:19 KJV

But prove yourselves doers of the word,
and not merely hearers who delude themselves.

James 1:22 NASB

For this is the love of God,
that we keep His commandments.
And His commandments are not burdensome.

I John 5:3 NKJV

About Putting God First

The most important thing you must decide
to do every day is put the Lord first.

ELIZABETH GEORGE

Christ is either Lord of all,
or He is not Lord at all.

HUDSON TAYLOR

God wants to be in our leisure time
as much as He is in our churches and in our work.

BETH MOORE

Even the most routine part of your day
can be a spiritual act of worship.

SARAH YOUNG

A Timely Tip

As you establish priorities for your day and your life, God deserves first place. And you deserve the experience of putting Him there.

33

God's Calling

A Prayer to Find My Calling

*I urge you to live a life worthy
of the calling you have received.*

Ephesians 4:1 NIV

Dear Lord, You have given me special talents and unique opportunities for service. I thank You for these gifts, which lead me along the path You have chosen.

You have called me, Father, and I will answer. I will study Your Word; I will seek Your guidance; and I will listen carefully to the quiet voice you have placed within my heart.

Give me the wisdom to know Your plan for my life and give me the courage to follow wherever You may lead me, Lord, today, tomorrow, and forever.

Amen

More from God's Word

But as God has distributed to each one,
as the Lord has called each one, so let him walk.

I CORINTHIANS 7:17 NKJV

For whoever does the will of God
is My brother and My sister and mother.

MARK 3:35 NKJV

For you have need of endurance,
so that when you have done the will of God,
you may receive what was promised.

HEBREWS 10:36 NASB

For many are called, but few are chosen.

MATTHEW 22:14 KJV

And we know that all things work together
for good to those who love God, to those who
are the called according to His purpose.

ROMANS 8:28 NKJV

About God's Calling

*God will help us become the people we are
meant to be, if only we will ask Him.*

HANNAH WHITALL SMITH

*God never calls a person into
His service without equipping him.*

BILLY GRAHAM

*All of God's people are ordinary people who have been
made extraordinary by the purpose He has given them.*

OSWALD CHAMBERS

*There's some task which the God of all the universe,
the great Creator, has for you to do, and which
will remain undone and incomplete until, by faith
and obedience, you step into the will of God.*

ALAN REDPATH

A Timely Tip

God has a plan for your life, a divine calling that
only you can fulfill. How you choose to respond to His
calling will determine the direction you take and the
contributions you make.

34

God's Faithfulness

Gratitude for God's Faithfulness

*Let us hold fast the confession of our hope
without wavering, for He who promised is faithful.*

Hebrews 10:23 NASB

Dear Lord, You have promised to be faithful. Thank You, Father, for Your steadfast love. Just as You have been faithful to me, let me be faithful to You, today and every day of my life. I have so many reasons to be grateful, and all my blessings come from You.

Today, Lord, I will rest in the knowledge of Your constant love for me. And I will serve You with willing hands and a loving heart.

Amen

More from God's Word

Great is thy faithfulness.

<small>LAMENTATIONS 3:23 KJV</small>

I will sing about the LORD's faithful love forever;
with my mouth I will proclaim
Your faithfulness to all generations.

<small>PSALM 89:1 HCSB</small>

For the LORD is good; His mercy is everlasting,
and His truth endures to all generations.

<small>PSALM 100:5 NKJV</small>

God, You are my God; I eagerly seek You.
I thirst for You. My lips will glorify You
because Your faithful love is better than life.

<small>PSALM 63:1, 3 HCSB</small>

God is faithful; by Him you were called
into fellowship with His Son, Jesus Christ our Lord.

<small>I CORINTHIANS 1:9 HCSB</small>

About God's Faithfulness

In God's faithfulness lies eternal security.

CORRIE TEN BOOM

There are four words I wish we would never forget, and they are, "God keeps his word."

CHARLES SWINDOLL

Trials are not enemies of faith but opportunities to reveal God's faithfulness.

BARBARA JOHNSON

Don't let obstacles along the road to eternity shake your confidence in God's promises.

DAVID JEREMIAH

A Timely Tip

Of this you can be sure: God's faithfulness is unwavering and eternal. Because He is faithful, you can—and should—live courageously.

35

God's Guidance

A Prayer for God's Guidance

Trust in the LORD with all your heart, and lean not on your own understanding; in all your ways acknowledge Him, and He shall direct your paths.

PROVERBS 3:5–6 NKJV

Heavenly Father, You have promised to guide me along a path of Your choosing. Today, I will listen carefully for Your voice as I seek Your guidance in every aspect of my life.

I will trust You to show me the path that I should take, and I will strive to follow as closely as I can in the footsteps of Your Son.

I draw near to You, Lord, with the confidence that You will lead me to a place of abundance. And as I make the journey, let me share Your good news with all who cross my path.

Amen

More from God's Word

Yet LORD, You are our Father;
we are the clay, and You are our potter;
we all are the work of Your hands.

ISAIAH 64:8 HCSB

Teach me to do Your will, for You are my God;
Your Spirit is good. Lead me in the land of uprightness.

PSALM 143:10 NKJV

Morning by morning he wakens me and opens my
understanding to his will. The Sovereign
LORD has spoken to me, and I have listened.

ISAIAH 50:4–5 NLT

Shew me thy ways, O LORD; teach me thy paths.
Lead me in thy truth, and teach me: for thou art
the God of my salvation; on thee do I wait all the day.

PSALM 25:4–5 KJV

The LORD says, "I will guide you along
the best pathway for your life.
I will advise you and watch over you."

PSALM 32:8 NLT

About God's Guidance

*God never leads us to do anything
that is contrary to the Bible.*

BILLY GRAHAM

*The will of God will never take us where
the grace of God cannot sustain us.*

BILLY GRAHAM

*Are you serious about wanting God's guidance
to become a personal reality in your life?
The first step is to tell God that you know you can't
manage your own life; that you need His help.*

CATHERINE MARSHALL

*When we are obedient,
God guides our steps and our stops.*

CORRIE TEN BOOM

A Timely Tip

If you want God's guidance, ask for it. When you pray for guidance, the Lord will give it. He will guide your steps if you let Him. Let Him.

36

God's Presence

In God's Presence

*For the eyes of Yahweh range throughout
the earth to show Himself strong
for those whose hearts are completely His.*

II Chronicles 16:9 HCSB

Dear Lord, You have promised to be with me always. Because I know that I'm never alone, I can face the challenges of this world with hope and assurance.

Heavenly Father, You are nearer to me than the air that I breathe. Help me feel Your presence in every situation and in every circumstance.

Today, Dear God, let me feel the presence of Your love, Your power, Your abundance, and Your Son.

Amen

More from God's Word

Be still, and know that I am God . . .

PSALM 46:10 KJV

I know the LORD is always with me.
I will not be shaken, for he is right beside me.

PSALM 16:8 NLT

I am not alone,
because the Father is with Me.

JOHN 16:32 NKJV

Though I walk through the valley
of the shadow of death, I will fear no evil:
for thou art with me.

PSALM 23:4 KJV

Draw near to God,
and He will draw near to you.

JAMES 4:8 HCSB

About God's Presence

*God is an infinite circle
whose center is everywhere.*

ST. AUGUSTINE

*The Lord is the one who travels
every mile of the wilderness way
as our leader, cheering us,
supporting and supplying and fortifying us.*

ELISABETH ELLIOT

*Do not limit the limitless God! With Him,
face the future unafraid because
you are never alone.*

LETTIE COWMAN

*Mark it down. You will never
go where God is not.*

MAX LUCADO

A Timely Tip

God isn't far away—He's right here, right now.
And He's willing to talk to you right here, right now.

37

God's Sufficiency

Recognizing God's Sufficiency

My grace is sufficient for you,
for my power is made perfect in weakness.

II CORINTHIANS 12:9 NIV

Dear Lord, You have promised that Your grace is sufficient to meet my every need. I trust Your promise, Father, and I thank You for Your guidance and protection.

I will turn to You, Lord, when I am anxious or fearful. You are my loving Heavenly Father, sufficient in all things; I will trust You always.

Today, I will entrust to You the challenges that are simply too big for me to solve. And with You by my side, I will be your confident servant, today, tomorrow, and forever.

Amen

More from God's Word

*And my God will supply all your needs according
to His riches in glory in Christ Jesus.*

PHILIPPIANS 4:19 HCSB

*And God is able to make every grace overflow to you,
so that in every way, always having everything
you need, you may excel in every good work.*

II CORINTHIANS 9:8 HCSB

*All of you, take up My yoke and learn from Me,
because I am gentle and humble in heart,
and you will find rest for yourselves.
For My yoke is easy and My burden is light.*

MATTHEW 11:29–30 HCSB

*The LORD is my strength and song, And He has become
my salvation; He is my God, and I will praise Him.*

EXODUS 15:2 NKJV

*For the eyes of the Lord are on the righteous,
and His ears are open to their prayers;
but the face of the Lord is against those who do evil.*

I PETER 3:12 NKJV

About God's Sufficiency

God is sufficient for all our needs, for every problem,
for every difficulty, for every broken heart,
for every human sorrow.

PETER MARSHALL

God often puts us in situations that are
too much for us so that we will learn
that no situation is too much for Him.

ERWIN LUTZER

God is trying to get a message through to you,
and the message is: "Stop depending on inadequate
human resources. Let me handle the matter."

CATHERINE MARSHALL

A Timely Tip

God is sufficient. Whatever you really need, He can provide. Whatever your weakness, He is stronger. And His strength will help you measure up to the tasks He intends for you to accomplish.

38

God's Timing

At Peace with God's Timing

*Therefore humble yourselves under the mighty hand
of God, that He may exalt you in due time.*

I Peter 5:6 NKJV

Heavenly Father, You have promised that when I am
patient, You will reward me in Your own way, at a time
of your choosing.

Your wisdom is infinite, Lord, and the timing of
Your heavenly plan is perfect for me. I will seek Your
guidance and trust Your plans for me today and every
day of my life.

When I am impatient, remind me that You are never early or late. You are always on time, Father, so let
me trust in You. Always.

Amen

More from God's Word

He has made everything appropriate in its time.
He has also put eternity in their hearts, but man cannot
discover the work God has done from beginning to end.

ECCLESIASTES 3:11 HCSB

Trust in the LORD with all your heart, and lean not
on your own understanding; in all your ways
acknowledge Him, and He shall direct your paths.

PROVERBS 3:5–6 NKJV

Those who trust in the LORD are like Mount Zion.
It cannot be shaken; it remains forever.

PSALM 125:1 HCSB

To every thing there is a season,
and a time to every purpose under the heaven.

ECCLESIASTES 3:1 KJV

Yet the LORD longs to be gracious to you; therefore he
will rise up to show you compassion. For the LORD
is a God of justice. Blessed are all who wait for him!

ISAIAH 30:18 NIV

About God's Timing

*We must learn to move according to the timetable
of the Timeless One, and to be at peace.*

ELISABETH ELLIOT

*We often hear about waiting on God,
which actually means that He is waiting until we
are ready. There is another side, however. When we
wait for God, we are waiting until He is ready.*

LETTIE COWMAN

*Teach us, O Lord, the disciplines of patience,
for to wait is often harder than to work.*

PETER MARSHALL

*The Christian's journey through life
isn't a sprint but a marathon.*

BILLY GRAHAM

A Timely Tip

Although you don't know precisely what you need—
or when you need it—God does. So trust His timing.

39

Hope

A Prayer for Hope

Let us hold fast the confession of our hope without wavering, for He who promised is faithful.

HEBREWS 10:23 NASB

Dear Lord, You have promised to be faithful. I am grateful for Your protection and Your love.

Because You watch over me, Lord, I have hope for the future and joy in my heart for the promise of eternal life.

Heavenly Father, let my hopes begin and end with You. When I am discouraged, I will turn to You. When I am weak, I will find strength in You. You are my rock and my strength. Today and every day, I will place my faith, my trust, and my hopes in You.

Amen

More from God's Word

This hope we have as an anchor of the soul,
a hope both sure and steadfast . . .

HEBREWS 6:19 NASB

The LORD is good to those who wait for Him,
To the soul who seeks Him.
It is good that one should hope and wait quietly
For the salvation of the LORD.

LAMENTATIONS 3:25–26 NKJV

Be strong and courageous,
all you who put your hope in the LORD.

PSALM 31:24 HCSB

Hope deferred makes the heart sick.

PROVERBS 13:12 NKJV

I say to myself, "The LORD is mine, so I hope in him."

LAMENTATIONS 3:24 NCV

About Hope

*The presence of hope in the invincible
sovereignty of God drives out fear.*

JOHN PIPER

*If your hopes are being disappointed just now,
it means that they are being purified.*

OSWALD CHAMBERS

The earth's troubles fade in the light of heaven's hope.

BILLY GRAHAM

*Jesus gives us hope because He keeps us company,
has a vision, and knows the way we should go.*

MAX LUCADO

A Timely Tip

If you're experiencing tough times, remember that other people have faced similar situations. They made it, and so can you. If you do your part, God will do His part. So never be afraid to hope—or to ask—for a miracle.

40

Humility

A Prayer for Humility

*Therefore humble yourselves under the mighty hand
of God, that He may exalt you in due time,
casting all your care upon Him, for He cares for you.*

I Peter 5:6–7 NKJV

Heavenly Father, Your Word teaches me to be humble. Yet the world tempts me to do otherwise. Help me guard my heart against the sin of pride.

Keep me humble, Lord. Let me grow beyond my need for earthly praise, and let me look only to You for approval. You are the Giver of all good gifts; let me give all the glory to You.

Jesus clothed Himself with humility. Today and every day, let me follow His example. Christ came to this earth so that He might live and die for us. Clothe me with humility, Lord, so that I might be more like Your Son.

Amen

More from God's Word

Always be humble, gentle, and patient,
accepting each other in love.

EPHESIANS 4:2 NCV

For everyone who exalts himself
will be humbled, and the one who
humbles himself will be exalted.

LUKE 14:11 HCSB

Blessed are the meek:
for they shall inherit the earth.

MATTHEW 5:5 KJV

Therefore, God's chosen ones, holy and loved,
put on heartfelt compassion, kindness,
humility, gentleness, and patience.

COLOSSIANS 3:12 HCSB

Humble yourselves in the sight of the Lord,
and he shall lift you up.

JAMES 4:10 KJV

About Humility

Pride builds walls between people,
humility builds bridges.

RICK WARREN

The holy man is the most humble man you can meet.

OSWALD CHAMBERS

God measures people by the small dimensions
of humility and not by the bigness of their
achievements or the size of their capabilities.

BILLY GRAHAM

Faith itself cannot be strong where humility is weak.

C. H. SPURGEON

A Timely Tip

God favors the humble just as surely as He disciplines the proud. Humility leads to contentment; pride doesn't. Act accordingly.

41

Judging Others

Judge Not

Judge not, and you shall not be judged.
Condemn not, and you shall not be condemned.
Forgive, and you will be forgiven.

Luke 6:37 NKJV

Father, sometimes, I am too quick to judge others. Keep me mindful that when I judge other people, I am living outside of Your will.

You have forgiven me, Lord. Let me be quick to forgive others.

Today, I ask that You cleanse my heart, Father, of bitterness and hatred. When other people harm me, let me forgive them, let me love them, and let me help them—without judging them.

Amen

More from God's Word

Don't criticize one another, brothers. He who criticizes
a brother or judges his brother criticizes the law
and judges the law. But if you judge the law,
you are not a doer of the law but a judge.

JAMES 4:11 HCSB

Do everything without grumbling and arguing,
so that you may be blameless and pure . . .

PHILIPPIANS 2:14–15 HCSB

Let the words of my mouth and the meditation
of my heart be acceptable in Your sight,
O LORD, my strength and my Redeemer.

PSALM 19:14 NKJV

Those who guard their lips preserve their lives,
but those who speak rashly will come to ruin.

PROVERBS 13:3 NIV

Therefore, any one of you who judges is without
excuse. For when you judge another, you condemn
yourself, since you, the judge, do the same things.

ROMANS 2:1 HCSB

About Judging Others

We must learn to regard people
less in the light of what they do or omit to do,
and more in light of what they suffer.

DIETRICH BONHOEFFER

Judging draws the judgment of others.

CATHERINE MARSHALL

Yes, let God be the Judge.
Your job today is to be a witness.

WARREN WIERSBE

Don't judge other people more harshly
than you want God to judge you.

MARIE T. FREEMAN

A Timely Tip

If you catch yourself being overly judgmental, slow
down long enough to interrupt those critical thoughts
before they hijack your emotions and wreck your day.

42

Listening to God

Praying for a Quiet Spirit

Be still, and know that I am God . . .

PSALM 46:10 KJV

Heavenly Father, I have so much to learn and You have so much to teach. Give me the wisdom to be still and the discernment to hear Your quiet voice, today and every day of my life.

I live in a noisy world, Lord, filled with distractions, interruptions, and temptations. Give me a quiet spirit, so I can listen carefully to the only guidance that really matters: Your guidance.

Amen

More from God's Word

In quietness and in confidence
shall be your strength.

<small>ISAIAH 30:15 KJV</small>

Listen, listen to me, and eat what is good,
and your soul will delight in the richest of fare.
Give ear and come to me; listen, that you may live.

<small>ISAIAH 55:2–3 NIV</small>

Be silent before Me . . .

<small>ISAIAH 41:1 HCSB</small>

The one who is from God listens to God's words.
This is why you don't listen,
because you are not from God.

<small>JOHN 8:47 HCSB</small>

Rest in the LORD, and wait patiently for Him.

<small>PSALM 37:7 NKJV</small>

About Listening to God

When God speaks to us,
He should have our full attention.

BILLY GRAHAM

God's voice is still and quiet
and easily buried under an avalanche of clamor.

CHARLES STANLEY

Prayer begins by talking to God,
but it ends in listening to Him. In the face of
Absolute Truth, silence is the soul's language.

FULTON J. SHEEN

Deep within the center of the soul is a chamber of peace
where God lives and where, if we will enter it and quiet
all the other sounds, we can hear His gentle whisper.

LETTIE COWMAN

A Timely Tip

If you want to have a meaningful conversation with God, don't make Him shout. Instead, go to a quiet place and listen. If you keep listening long enough and carefully enough, the Lord will talk directly to you.

43

Miracles

Praying for a Miracle

Is anything too hard for the LORD?

GENESIS 18:14 NKJV

Dear Lord, You have promised that nothing, absolutely nothing, is impossible for You. You created the universe and You created me. Keep me mindful of Your strength.

Because Your power is limitless, I know that You perform miracles when it serves Your purpose. So today, I will open my eyes—and my heart—to watch for miracles. Because You love me, Father, and have promised to protect me, I will never lose hope.

Amen

More from God's Word

God confirmed the message by signs and wonders
and various miracles and gifts
of the Holy Spirit whenever he chose.

HEBREWS 2:4 NLT

You are the God of miracles and wonders!
You demonstrate your awesome power
among the nations.

PSALM 77:14 NLT

For with God nothing shall be impossible.

LUKE 1:37 KJV

And Jesus looking upon them saith,
With men it is impossible, but not with God:
for with God all things are possible.

MARK 10:27 KJV

What no eye has seen, what no ear has heard,
and what no human mind has conceived the things
God has prepared for those who love him.

I CORINTHIANS 2:9 NIV

About Miracles

God specializes in things thought impossible.

CATHERINE MARSHALL

*God's specialty is raising dead things to life
and making impossible things possible.
You don't have the need that exceeds His power.*

BETH MOORE

*Are you looking for a miracle?
If you keep your eyes wide open and trust in God,
you won't have to look very far.*

MARIE T. FREEMAN

God is able to do what we can't do.

BILLY GRAHAM

A Timely Tip

Nothing is impossible for God. And He's in the business of doing miraculous things. So, never be afraid to ask for a miracle.

44

Opportunities

Making the Most of Opportunities

But as it is written: What no eye has seen
and no ear has heard, and what has never come
into a man's heart, is what God has
prepared for those who love Him.

I CORINTHIANS 2:9 HCSB

Dear Lord, as I take the next steps on my journey, I will take them with You. Whatever this day may hold for me, I will thank You for the opportunity to live joyfully and abundantly. Let me lean upon You, Lord—and trust You—now and forever.

Make my work pleasing to You, Father, and help me to sow the seeds of kindness everywhere I go. Let me be passionate about my opportunities and responsibilities. And give me wisdom to wait patiently for success to come my way.

Amen

More from God's Word

But those who wait on the L<small>ORD</small>
Shall renew their strength;
They shall mount up with wings like eagles,
They shall run and not be weary,
They shall walk and not faint.

<small>ISAIAH 40:31</small> NKJV

I can do all things through Christ
which strengtheneth me.

<small>PHILIPPIANS 4:13</small> KJV

I remind you to fan into flame the gift of God . . .

<small>II TIMOTHY 1:6</small> NIV

Remember ye not the former things,
neither consider the things of old.
Behold, I will do a new thing . . .

<small>ISAIAH 43:18–19</small> KJV

Whenever we have the opportunity,
we should do good to everyone,
especially to in the family of faith.

<small>GALATIANS 6:10</small> NLT

About Opportunities

We are all faced with a series
of great opportunities brilliantly disguised
as impossible situations.

CHARLES SWINDOLL

A possibility is a hint from God.

SØREN KIERKEGAARD

The past is our teacher;
the present is our opportunity;
the future is our friend.

EDWIN LOUIS COLE

Each day is God's gift of a fresh,
unspoiled opportunity to live
according to His priorities.

ELIZABETH GEORGE

A Timely Tip

God constantly arrives at our doorsteps with countless opportunities. And He knocks. Our challenge, of course, is to open the door.

45

Past

Making Peace with the Past

*Do not remember the former things, nor consider
the things of old. Behold, I will do a new thing.*

ISAIAH 43:18–19 NKJV

Dear Lord, help me live in the present, not the past.
When I am bitter or resentful, I cannot feel Your peace.
So help me accept the past, treasure the present, and
entrust the future to You.

You have promised that each day is a gift. Help me
spend this day—and every day—in the precious present,
not the unchangeable past. And let me share the good
news of Your Son so that others, too, might receive
His eternal gifts.

Amen

More from God's Word

One thing I do, forgetting those things which are behind and reaching forward to those things which are ahead, I press toward the goal for the prize of the upward call of God in Christ Jesus.

PHILIPPIANS 3:13–14 NKJV

For you died to this life, and your real life is hidden with Christ in God.

COLOSSIANS 3:3 NCV

And He who sits on the throne said, "Behold, I am making all things new."

REVELATION 21:5 NASB

He restoreth my soul: he leadeth me in the paths of righteousness for his name's sake.

PSALM 23:3 KJV

Have mercy on me, O God, according to your unfailing love; according to your great compassion blot out my transgressions. Wash away all my iniquity and cleanse me from my sin.

PSALM 51:1–2 NIV

The Past

Don't waste energy regretting
the way things are or thinking
about what might have been.
Start at the present moment—
accepting things exactly as they are—
and search for My way in the midst
of those circumstances.

SARAH YOUNG

Don't be bound by the past and its failures.
But don't forget its lessons either.

BILLY GRAHAM

Trust the past to God's mercy, the present
to God's love, and the future to God's providence.

ST. AUGUSTINE

A Timely Tip

The past is past. Don't invest all your mental energy there. If you're focusing on yesterday, it's time to change your focus. And if you're living in the past, move on while there's still time.

46

Patience

Praying for Patience

A person's wisdom yields patience;
it is to his glory to overlook an offense.

Proverbs 19:11 NIV

Heavenly Father, Your Word promises that patience is rewarded. And I trust that promise, so I ask that You help me gain the wisdom to be patient.

Today, I will live according to Your plan and according to Your timetable. And I will wait quietly for You, Father.

When I am hurried, slow me down. When I become impatient with others, give me empathy. Today, let me be a patient Christian as I trust in You, Father, and in Your master plan for my life.

Amen

More from God's Word

Patience of spirit is better than haughtiness of spirit.

ECCLESIASTES 7:8 NASB

But if we hope for what we do not yet have,
we wait for it patiently.

ROMANS 8:25 NIV

The LORD is wonderfully good
to those who wait for him and seek him.
So it is good to wait quietly
for salvation from the LORD.

LAMENTATIONS 3:25–26 NLT

Be joyful in hope,
patient in affliction,
faithful in prayer.

ROMANS 12:12 NIV

It is better to be patient than powerful;
it is better to have self-control than to conquer a city.

PROVERBS 16:32 NLT

About Patience

Patience is the companion of wisdom.

ST. AUGUSTINE

Frustration is not the will of God.
There is time to do anything
and everything that God wants us to do.

ELISABETH ELLIOT

Today, take a complicated situation and with time,
patience, and a smile, turn it into something positive—
for you and for others.

JONI EARECKSON TADA

Patience graciously, compassionately,
and with understanding judges the faults
of others without unjust criticism.

BILLY GRAHAM

A Timely Tip

When you learn to be a more patient person, you'll
make your world—and your heart—a better place.

47

Peace

Praying for a Peaceful Heart

Peace I leave with you, My peace I give to you;
not as the world gives do I give to you.
Let not your heart be troubled, neither let it be afraid.

John 14:27 NKJV

Heavenly Father, You have promised that I can experience Your peace. And I thank You for that gift.

The peace that the world offers is fleeting, but You offer a peace that is perfect and eternal.

Today, let me experience the spiritual abundance that You offer through Your Son, the Prince of Peace. He gives me a sense of peace that the world can never offer. I thank You, Father, for Your love, for Your peace, and for Your Son.

Amen

More from God's Word

For He Himself is our peace.

EPHESIANS 2:14 NASB

But the fruit of the Spirit is love, joy,
peace, patience, kindness, goodness,
faith, gentleness, self-control.
Against such things there is no law.

GALATIANS 5:22–23 HCSB

These things I have spoken to you, that in Me
you may have peace. In the world
you will have tribulation; but be of good cheer,
I have overcome the world.

JOHN 16:33 NKJV

"I will give peace, real peace,
to those far and near,
and I will heal them," says the LORD.

ISAIAH 57:19 NCV

The peace of God, which passeth all understanding,
shall keep your hearts and minds through Christ Jesus.

PHILIPPIANS 4:7 KJV

About Peace

Deep within the center of the soul
is a chamber of peace where God lives and where,
if we will enter it and quiet all the other sounds,
we can hear His gentle whisper.

LETTIE COWMAN

God's power is great enough for our deepest
desperation. You can go on. You can pick up the pieces
and start anew. You can face your fears. You can find
peace in the rubble. There is healing for your soul.

SUZANNE DALE EZELL

Peace does not mean to be in a place where there is no
noise, trouble, or hard work. Peace means to be in the
midst of all those things and still be calm in your heart.

CATHERINE MARSHALL

A Timely Tip

Sometimes peace can be a scarce commodity in a noisy, complicated, twenty-first-century world. But God's peace is always available when you turn everything over to Him.

48

Perseverance

A Prayer for the Strength to Persevere

*Let us not become weary in doing good,
for at the proper time we will reap
a harvest if we do not give up.*

GALATIANS 6:9 NIV

Heavenly Father, You have promised that my perseverance will be rewarded. But when I experience the inevitable hardships of life, I am tempted to abandon hope.

I can draw strength from You, Lord, in good times and hard times. Let me persevere—even if my soul is troubled—and let me follow Your Son, now and forever.

Today, Father, I will be a finisher of my faith. Even if the day is difficult, I will do the work You have placed before me. And I will strive to follow Your Son this day and forever.

Amen

More from God's Word

But as for you, be strong; don't be discouraged,
for your work has a reward.

II Chronicles 15:7 HCSB

Finishing is better than starting.
Patience is better than pride.

Ecclesiastes 7:8 NLT

So let us run the race that is before us
and never give up. We should remove
from our lives anything that would get in the way
and the sin that so easily holds us back.

Hebrews 12:1 NCV

For you have need of endurance,
so that when you have done the will of God,
you may receive what was promised.

Hebrews 10:36 NASB

We are hard-pressed on every side,
yet not crushed; we are perplexed,
but not in despair.

II Corinthians 4:8 NKJV

About Perseverance

Perseverance is more than endurance.
It is endurance combined with absolute assurance
and certainty that what we are
looking for is going to happen.

OSWALD CHAMBERS

Success or failure can be pretty well predicted
by the degree to which the heart is fully in it.

JOHN ELDREDGE

Patience and diligence,
like faith, remove mountains.

WILLIAM PENN

Everyone gets discouraged. The question is:
Are you going to give up or get up? It's a choice.

JOHN MAXWELL

A Timely Tip

Life is, at times, difficult. When you are tested, don't quit at the first sign of trouble. Instead, call upon God. He can give you the strength to persevere, and that's exactly what you should ask Him to do.

49

Pleasing God

A Prayer about Pleasing God

*For it is not merely knowing the law
that brings God's approval. Those who obey the law
will be declared right in God's sight.*

Romans 2:13 NLT

Dear Lord, You have promised that You are pleased by my obedience. Today, Lord, I will strive to please You; I will strive to serve You; and I will strive to obey Your commandments.

Your blessings are as limitless as Your love. I will worship You, Father, with my words, my prayers, and my deeds.

Your commandments are a perfect guide for my life; let me obey them and help others do the same. And give me the wisdom to walk righteously, Dear Heavenly Father, with You every day of my life.

Amen

More from God's Word

*Our only goal is to please God
whether we live here or there, because we must
all stand before Christ to be judged.*

II Corinthians 5:9–10 NCV

*Give to the Lord the glory due His name;
bring an offering, and come into His courts.*

Psalm 96:8 NKJV

*Obviously, I'm not trying to win the approval
of people, but of God. If pleasing people were my goal,
I would not be Christ's servant.*

Galatians 1:10 NLT

*And it is impossible to please God without faith.
Anyone who wants to come to him
must believe that God exists and that he
rewards those who sincerely seek him.*

Hebrews 11:6 NLT

*But prove yourselves doers of the word,
and not merely hearers who delude themselves.*

James 1:22 NASB

About Pleasing God

*An ongoing relationship with God through His Word
is essential to the Christian's consistent victory.*

BETH MOORE

*We may blunder on for years thinking we know a great
deal about Him, and then, perhaps suddenly,
we catch a sight of Him as He is revealed in the face
of Jesus Christ, and we discover the real God.*

HANNAH WHITALL SMITH

*Give me grace ever to desire and to will what is most
acceptable to thee and most pleasing in thy sight.*

THOMAS À KEMPIS

*Loving God—really loving Him—means living out
His commands no matter what the cost.*

CHARLES COLSON

A Timely Tip

Being obedient to God means that you can't always please other people. So focus, first and foremost, on your relationship with the Creator. When you do, you'll find that every other relationship and every other aspect of your life will be more fulfilling.

50

Possibilities

Praying about the Possibilities

But Jesus looked at them and said to them,
"With men this is impossible,
but with God all things are possible."

MATTHEW 19:26 NKJV

Dear Lord, Jesus promised that nothing is impossible for You. So I will never lose hope in Your ability to guide my steps and transform my life.

You have a plan for me, Father. Help me consider my possibilities and discover my calling. And as I seek Your purpose for my life, give me the wisdom to trust You completely.

Today, I will strive to live courageously as I place my hopes, my faith, and my life in Your hands, Lord. Let my life be a testimony to the transforming power of Your love and Your Son.

Amen

More from God's Word

*I can do all things
through Christ which strengtheneth me.*

PHILIPPIANS 4:13 KJV

*The things which are impossible with men
are possible with God.*

LUKE 18:27 KJV

Is anything too hard for the LORD?

GENESIS 18:14 KJV

*Therefore we do not lose heart.
Even though our outward man is perishing,
yet the inward man is being renewed day by day.*

II CORINTHIANS 4:16 NKJV

*Jesus said to him, "If you can believe,
all things are possible to him who believes."*

MARK 9:23 NKJV

About Possibilities

*God's specialty is raising dead things to life
and making impossible things possible.
You don't have the need that exceeds His power.*

BETH MOORE

*We are all faced with a series of great opportunities
brilliantly disguised as impossible situations.*

CHARLES SWINDOLL

*Alleged "impossibilities" are opportunities
for our capacities to be stretched.*

CHARLES SWINDOLL

A possibility is a hint from God.

SØREN KIERKEGAARD

A Timely Tip

God has no limits. With Him, all things are possible. As you consider your possibilities and your plans, remember to make your Heavenly Father a full partner in every endeavor.

51

Priorities

Praying about Priorities

Therefore, whether you eat or drink,
or whatever you do, do everything for God's glory.

I Corinthians 10:31 HCSB

Heavenly Father, let Your priorities be my priorities. Let Your will be my will. Let Your Word be my guide, and let me grow in my faith this day and every day.

This day, like every other, is both a gift and an opportunity. Help me finish the important tasks first, even if those tasks are unpleasant. Give me the wisdom and the courage to do what needs to be done, when it needs to be done. And let me teach others to do the same.

Amen

More from God's Word

Trust in the Lord with all your heart
and lean not on your own understanding.

PROVERBS 3:5 NIV

But prove yourselves doers of the word,
and not merely hearers who delude themselves.

JAMES 1:22 NASB

He who trusts in his riches will fall,
but the righteous will flourish . . .

PROVERBS 11:28 NASB

For where your treasure is,
there your heart will be also.

LUKE 12:34 HCSB

Set an example of good works yourself,
with integrity and dignity in your teaching.

TITUS 2:7 HCSB

About Priorities

Energy and time are limited entities.
Therefore, we need to use them wisely,
focusing on what is truly important.

Sarah Young

Put first things first and we get second things
thrown in; put second things first
and we lose both first and second things.

Elizabeth George

A disciple is a follower of Christ.
That means you take on His priorities as your own.
His agenda becomes your agenda.
His mission becomes your mission.

Charles Stanley

A Timely Tip

As you prioritize your day, ask God to help you sort out big responsibilities from small ones, major problems from minor ones, and important responsibilities from irrelevant ones. And if you're faced with a big decision, let God help you decide.

52

Problems

Praying about Problems

People who do what is right may have many problems,
but the LORD will solve them all.

PSALM 34:19 NCV

Dear Lord, this world can be a difficult place. When I encounter troubles that leave me worried and perplexed, I am tempted to lose hope. But Your Word promises that no problem is too big for You. Your promise gives me the confidence I need to persevere, even with I'm afraid.

When I am discouraged, Father, give me the wisdom to trust Your promises and the strength to follow Your will. Then, when I have done my best, let me live with the assurance that You are firmly in control, and that Your love endures forever.

Amen

More from God's Word

Consider it a great joy, my brothers, whenever you experience various trials, knowing that the testing of your faith produces endurance. But endurance must do its complete work, so that you may be mature and complete, lacking nothing.

James 1:2–4

Trust the LORD your God with all your heart and lean not on your own understanding; in all your ways acknowledge him, and he will make your paths straight.

Proverbs 3:5–6 NIV

I have learned in whatever state I am, to be content.

Philippians 4:11 NKJV

We are pressured in every way but not crushed; we are perplexed but not in despair.

II Corinthians 4:8 HCSB

We also have joy with our troubles, because we know that these troubles produce patience. And patience produces character, and character produces hope.

Romans 5:3–4 NCV

About Problems

*Human problems are never
greater than divine solutions.*

ERWIN LUTZER

*Faith points us beyond our problems
to the hope we have in Christ.*

BILLY GRAHAM

*Each problem is a
God-appointed instructor.*

CHARLES SWINDOLL

A Timely Tip

Most problems aren't self-solving. So if you want to
make them disappear, you'll need to spend more time
praying about your problems—and working to resolve
them—and less time fretting about them.

53

Purpose

A Prayer to Understand My Purpose

We have also received an inheritance in Him,
predestined according to the purpose
of the One who works out everything
in agreement with the decision of His will.

EPHESIANS 1:11 HCSB

Heavenly Father, You have promised that You have a plan for my life. I will trust Your promise, Lord, and I will continually strive to understand that plan.

As I seek to live a meaningful life, I will turn to You to find that meaning. Give me Your blessings, Father, and lead me along a path that is pleasing to You, today, tomorrow, and forever.

Dear Lord, You are the Creator of the universe, and I know that Your plan for my life is grander than I can imagine. Let Your purposes be my purposes, and let me trust in the assurance of Your promises.

Amen

More from God's Word

Whatever you eat or drink,
or whatever you do, do it all for the glory of God.

I Corinthians 10:31 NLT

For we are His creation, created in Christ Jesus
for good works, which God prepared ahead
of time so that we should walk in them.

Ephesians 2:10 HCSB

And whatever you do, do it heartily,
as to the Lord and not to men.

Colossians 3:23 NKJV

We must do the works of Him who sent Me while
it is day. Night is coming when no one can work.

John 9:4 HCSB

For we are God's coworkers.
You are God's field, God's building.

I Corinthians 3:9 HCSB

About Purpose

*The easiest way to discover the purpose of
an invention is to ask the creator of it. The same is true
for discovering your life's purpose: Ask God.*

RICK WARREN

*There's some task which the God of all the universe,
the great Creator, has for you to do, and which will
remain undone and incomplete until, by faith
and obedience, you step into the will of God.*

ALAN REDPATH

*You weren't an accident. You weren't mass-produced.
You aren't an assembly-line product. You were
deliberately planned, specifically gifted, and lovingly
positioned on the Earth by the Master Craftsman.*

MAX LUCADO

A Timely Tip

God has big things in store for you, but He may
have quite a few lessons to teach you before you are
fully prepared to fulfill His purposes. So be patient, be
watchful, keep working, and keep praying. Divine help
is on the way.

54

Renewal

A Prayer for Renewal

*Therefore, if anyone is in Christ,
he is a new creation; old things have passed away;
behold, all things have become new.*

II Corinthians 5:17 NKJV

Heavenly Father, You have promised to renew my spirit and restore my strength. You are my rock and my strength, Lord. Let me always trust Your promises, and let me draw strength from Your promises and from Your unending love.

Give me a fresh start and a new heart—a heart that reflects Your love. When I need to change, Lord, give me the wisdom to seek Your guidance and the courage to follow in the footsteps of Your Son.

Amen

More from God's Word

You are being renewed in the spirit of your minds;
you put on the new self, the one created according to
God's likeness in righteousness and purity of the truth.

Ephesians 4:23–24 HCSB

Remember ye not the former things, neither consider
the things of old. Behold, I will do a new thing . . .

Isaiah 43:18–19 KJV

Now the God of all grace, who called you to His
eternal glory in Christ Jesus, will personally restore,
establish, strengthen, and support you.

I Peter 5:10 HCSB

Finally, brothers, rejoice. Be restored,
be encouraged, be of the same mind, be at peace,
and the God of love and peace will be with you.

II Corinthians 13:11 HCSB

Those who hope in the Lord will renew their strength.
They will soar on wings like eagles; they will run
and not grow weary, they will walk and not be faint.

Isaiah 40:31 NIV

About Renewal

God specializes in giving people a fresh start.

RICK WARREN

Our Lord never drew power from Himself;
He drew it always from His Father.

OSWALD CHAMBERS

Are you weak? Weary? Confused? Troubled?
Pressured? How is your relationship with God?
Is it held in its place of priority?
I believe the greater the pressure,
the greater your need for time alone with Him.

KAY ARTHUR

The creation of a new heart, the renewing
of a right spirit is an omnipotent work of God.
Leave it to the Creator.

HENRY DRUMMOND

A Timely Tip

God can make all things new, including you. When you are weak or worried, He can renew your spirit and restore your strength. Your job, of course, is to let Him.

55

Serving God

Praying for a Servant's Heart

But he who is greatest among you must be a servant.
And whoever exalts himself will be humbled,
and he who humbles himself will be exalted.

MATTHEW 23:11–12 NKJV

Heavenly Father, the Bible teaches me to be a servant. I will trust Your Holy Word and honor You through my service to others.

When Jesus humbled Himself and became a servant, He also became an example for me. Make me a faithful steward of my gifts, and let me be a humble servant to my loved ones, to my friends, and to those in need.

Today, I ask that You give me a servant's heart. When I lose sight of Your purpose for my life, give me a passion for my daily responsibilities. And when I have completed my work, let all the honor and glory be Yours.

Amen

More from God's Word

Shepherd God's flock, for whom you are responsible.
Watch over them because you want to,
not because you are forced. That is how God wants it.
Do it because you are happy to serve.

I Peter 5:2 NCV

Blessed are those servants, whom the lord
when he cometh shall find watching . . .

Luke 12:37 KJV

Even so faith, if it hath not works,
is dead, being alone.

James 2:17 KJV

Assuredly, I say to you,
inasmuch as you did it to one of the least of these
My brethren, you did it to Me.

Matthew 25:40 NKJV

As each one has received a gift,
minister it to one another,
as good stewards of the manifold grace of God.

I Peter 4:10 NKJV

About Serving God

*Our voices, our service, and our abilities
are to be employed, primarily, for the glory of God.*

BILLY GRAHAM

*God wants us to serve Him with a willing spirit,
one that would choose no other way.*

BETH MOORE

*Faithful servants never retire.
You can retire from your career,
but you will never retire from serving God.*

RICK WARREN

*Your attitude of serving the Lord
can transform even the most menial of tasks
into a magnificent sacrifice of love.*

ELIZABETH GEORGE

A Timely Tip

God wants you to serve Him now, not later. So don't put off until tomorrow the good works you can perform for Him today.

56

Spiritual Growth

A Prayer for Spiritual Growth

*I remind you to fan into flames
the spiritual gift God gave you . . .*

II Timothy 1:6 NLT

Dear Lord, I want to grow closer to You each day. I know that obedience strengthens my relationship with You, so I ask You to help me follow Your will and obey Your Word.

I thank You, Father, for the opportunity to walk with Your Son. And I thank You for the opportunity to follow in His footsteps each day.

You sent Jesus so that I might have abundant life and eternal life. Thank You, Lord, for my Savior. I will follow Him, honor Him, and share His good news, this day and every day of my life.

Amen

More from God's Word

But endurance must do its complete work,
so that you may be mature and complete,
lacking nothing.

JAMES 1:4 HCSB

And be not conformed to this world:
but be ye transformed by the renewing of your mind,
that ye may prove what is that good,
and acceptable, and perfect will of God.

ROMANS 12:2 KJV

So let us stop going over the basics about Christ
again and again. Let us go on instead
and become mature in our understanding.

HEBREWS 6:1 NLT

Leave inexperience behind, and you will live;
pursue the way of understanding.

PROVERBS 9:6 HCSB

But grow in the grace and knowledge of our Lord
and Savior Jesus Christ. To Him be the glory
both now and forever. Amen.

II PETER 3:18 NKJV

About Spiritual Growth

Grow, dear friends, but grow, I beseech you,
in God's way, which is the only true way.

HANNAH WHITALL SMITH

God's ultimate goal for your life on earth
is not comfort, but character development. He wants
you to grow up spiritually and become like Christ.

RICK WARREN

The vigor of our spiritual life will be
in exact proportion to the place held
by the Bible in our life and thoughts.

GEORGE MUELLER

Mark it down. You will never go where God is not.

MAX LUCADO

A Timely Tip

When it comes to your faith, God doesn't want you
to stand still. He wants you to keep growing. He knows
that spiritual maturity is a journey, not a destination.
You should know it too.

170

57

Stress

A Prayer for Managing Stress

*Come unto me, all ye that labor and are heavy laden,
and I will give you rest.*

MATTHEW 11:28 KJV

Dear Lord, this world can be a stressful place, filled with too many distractions, too many temptations, and too many obligations. But Your Word promises that I can experience the peace that passes all understanding when I follow in the footsteps of Your Son. I thank You for Jesus and for the rest that I can find in Him.

When I am weighed down by the demands of the day, Lord, I know that You are always with me, protecting me from harm and encouraging me to persevere. So whatever this day may bring, I thank You for Your love, for Your strength, for Your protection, and for Your Son.

Amen

More from God's Word

And the peace of God, which transcends
all understanding, will guard your hearts
and your minds in Christ Jesus.

PHILIPPIANS 4:7 NIV

Peace I leave with you; My peace I give to you;
not as the world gives do I give to you.
Do not let your heart be troubled, nor let it be fearful.

JOHN 14:27 NASB

Live peaceful and quiet lives
in all godliness and holiness.

I TIMOTHY 2:2 NIV

You, LORD, give true peace to those who
depend on you, because they trust you.

ISAIAH 26:3 NCV

I find rest in God; only he gives me hope.

PSALM 62:5 NCV

About Stress

Life is strenuous. See that your
clock does not run down.

Lettie Cowman

The more comfortable we are with mystery in our
journey, the more rest we will know along the way.

John Eldredge

God specializes in giving people a fresh start.

Rick Warren

Beware of having so much to do
that you really do nothing at all
because you do not wait upon God to do it right.

C. H. Spurgeon

A Timely Tip

With God as your partner, you can overcome any obstacle. When you place your future in His hands, you have absolutely nothing to fear. The more you pray, the less stress you'll feel. So pray more and worry less.

58

Today

A Prayer about Today

This is the day the LORD has made;
let us rejoice and be glad in it.

PSALM 118:24 HCSB

Dear Lord, You have given me this day, yet another opportunity to celebrate the gift of life as I follow in the footsteps of Your Son.

You have promised that heaven is eternal. But I am only here on Earth for a few short years. So let me use my time wisely.

Enable me to live this day to the fullest, totally involved in Your will. And when the day is done, let me say another prayer of thanks for the precious gift of life.

Amen

More from God's Word

But encourage each other every day while it is "today."
Help each other so none of you will become hardened
because sin has tricked you.

HEBREWS 3:13 NCV

There is a time for everything, and a season
for every activity under the heavens.

ECCLESIASTES 3:1 NIV

So teach us to number our days,
that we may present to You a heart of wisdom.

PSALM 90:12 NASB

The world and its desires pass away,
but whoever does the will of God lives forever.

I JOHN 2:17 NIV

So don't worry about tomorrow,
because tomorrow will have its own worries.
Each day has enough trouble of its own.

MATTHEW 6:34 NCV

About Today

*Yesterday is the tomb of time, and tomorrow
is the womb of time. Only now is yours.*

R. G. LEE

*Faith does not concern itself with the entire journey.
One step is enough.*

LETTIE COWMAN

*Each day is God's gift of a fresh, unspoiled
opportunity to live according to His priorities.*

ELIZABETH GEORGE

*Today is mine. Tomorrow is none of my business.
If I peer anxiously into the fog of the future,
I will strain my spiritual eyes so that I
will not see clearly what is required of me now.*

ELISABETH ELLIOT

A Timely Tip

Every day is a beautifully wrapped gift from God.
Unwrap it, and give thanks to the Giver.

59

Trusting God

Trusting God

*Trust in the LORD with all your heart, and lean not
on your own understanding; in all your ways
acknowledge Him, and He shall direct your paths.*

PROVERBS 3:5–6 NKJV

Dear Lord, You are my shepherd, my protector, and my guide. I will trust You, Father, today and every day. I will turn all my worries, all my anxieties, and all my concerns over to You. I will trust Your wisdom, Your plan, Your Promises, and Your Son.

I will trust You, Father, in every circumstance and in every stage of life because I know that every good gift comes from You. And I know that because of Your love, I am eternally blessed.

Amen

More from God's Word

In quietness and trust is your strength.

ISAIAH 30:15 NASB

The fear of man is a snare,
but the one who trusts in the LORD is protected.

PROVERBS 29:25 HCSB

Jesus said, "Don't let your hearts be troubled.
Trust in God, and trust in me."

JOHN 14:1 NCV

Those who trust in the LORD are like Mount Zion.
It cannot be shaken; it remains forever.

PSALM 125:1 HCSB

The LORD is my rock, my fortress,
and my deliverer, my God,
my mountain where I seek refuge.
My shield, the horn of my salvation,
my stronghold, my refuge, and my Savior.

II SAMUEL 22:2–3 HCSB

About Trusting God

*One of the marks of spiritual maturity is the quiet
confidence that God is in control, without the need
to understand why He does what He does.*

CHARLES SWINDOLL

*Never be afraid to trust an unknown
future to a known God.*

CORRIE TEN BOOM

*When a train goes through a tunnel and it gets dark,
you don't throw away your ticket and jump off.
You sit still and trust the engineer.*

CORRIE TEN BOOM

*Faith and obedience are bound up in
the same bundle. He that obeys God, trusts God;
and he that trusts God, obeys God.*

C. H. SPURGEON

A Timely Tip

Because God is trustworthy—and because He has
made promises to you that He intends to keep—you
are protected. The Lord always keeps His promises.
Trust Him.

60

Wisdom and Understanding

A Prayer for Wisdom and Understanding

The fear of the LORD is the beginning of knowledge,
but fools despise wisdom and instruction.

PROVERBS 1:7 NKJV

Dear Lord, the Bible instructs me to acquire wisdom. And I know that the ultimate wisdom is found on the pages of Your Holy Word. So I will study Your teachings and honor them with clear thoughts, with sincere prayers, and with an obedient heart.

I ask that You guide me, Father. Let me seek Your wisdom—and live by it—every day of my life.

When I trust in the wisdom of the world, I am often led astray, but when I trust You, Lord, I build my life upon a firm foundation. So I will trust in You now, and I will trust You forever.

Amen

More from God's Word

Acquire wisdom—how much better it is than gold!
And acquire understanding—it is preferable to silver.

PROVERBS 16:16 HCSB

He that walketh with wise men shall be wise:
but a companion of fools shall be destroyed.

PROVERBS 13:20 KJV

Who among you is wise and understanding?
Let him show by his good behavior
his deeds in the gentleness of wisdom.

JAMES 3:13 NASB

But if any of you lacks wisdom, let him ask of God,
who gives to all generously and without reproach,
and it will be given to him.

JAMES 1:5 NASB

But the wisdom that is from above is first pure, then
peaceable, gentle, willing to yield, full of mercy and
good fruits, without partiality and without hypocrisy.

JAMES 3:17 NKJV

About Wisdom

Wisdom is the right use of knowledge.
To know is not to be wise. There is no fool
so great as the knowing fool. But to know
how to use knowledge is to have wisdom.

C. H. SPURGEON

Wisdom is the power to see
and the inclination
to choose the best and highest goal,
together with the surest means of attaining it.

J. I. PACKER

True wisdom is marked by willingness
to listen and a sense of knowing
when to yield.

ELIZABETH GEORGE

A Timely Tip

Wisdom begins with a thorough understanding of God's moral order, the eternal truths that are found in His Holy Word. Real wisdom is more than mere knowledge. It's the application of God's truth in everyday life.